Pan ... and Me

ALSO BY MICHAEL J. ROADS

Nonfiction

Entering the Secret World of Nature

From Illusion to Enlightenment

Insights of a Modern Mystic

Talking with Nature—Journey into Nature

Journey into Oneness—Into a Timeless Realm

Stepping . . . Between . . . Realities

Through the Eyes of Love, Journeying with Pan, Book One

Through the Eyes of Love, Journeying with Pan, Book Two

Through the Eyes of Love, Journeying with Pan, Book Three

Conscious Gardening: Practical and Metaphysical Expert Advice to Grow Your Garden Organically

The Magic Formula

More Than Money –True Prosperity

A Glimpse of Something Greater

Fiction

Getting There

Award-winning and best-selling author of
Talking with Nature and *Journey into Nature*

Pan . . . and Me

Metaphysical Adventures with the Spirit of Nature

MICHAEL J. ROADS

SIX DEGREES PUBLISHING GROUP
Portland Oregon

Six Degrees Publishing Group
5331 S. Macadam Avenue, Suite 258
Portland, Oregon 97239 USA

www.sixdegreespublishing.com

PAN AND ME. Copyright © 2023 by Michael J. Roads. All rights reserved under International and Pan-American Copyright Conventions, the United Kingdom Copyright, Designs and Patents Act of 1988, and the US Copyright Act of 1976 and all amendments thereto. No part of this publication may be reproduced, distributed, or transmitted in any form or by any means, including photocopying, recording, or other electronic or mechanical methods, without the prior written permission of the publisher, except in the case of brief quotations embodied in critical reviews and certain other noncommercial uses permitted by copyright law.

For information and permissions please contact the publisher by email at: Publisher@SixDegreesPublishing.com

Print ISBN: 978-1-942497-54-7 | eISBN: 978-1-942497-55-4

PUBLISHER'S NOTE: This book is written in Australian English. Websites and email addresses contained in this book are current at the time of publication but may change or disappear at any time.

TRADEMARKS: Six Degrees Publishing Group and the Six Degrees Publishing Group colophon are trademarks of Six Degrees Publishing Group, Inc. and/or its affiliates in the United States and other countries and may not be used without written permission. Six Degrees Publishing Group is not associated with any product, vendor, or group in this book.

Cover Photo: Henry Watts @WattsinFocus

Published in the United States of America
Printed simultaneously in the United States of America,
the United Kingdom and Australia

FIRST PAPERBACK EDITION 2023

1 3 5 7 9 10 8 6 4 2

Dedication

This is an extract from an email from Jimmy—Carolyn's ex-husband and continuing good friend—who had been hiking with two buddies, Alan and Herman. Alan has known Carolyn all his life.

"So Alan was telling Herman, *I know you never knew Carolyn, but let me put it like this: being with her is like the closest thing to being with God.*

"I swear that's what he said. It was nine in the morning. No one had been drinking!"

What more can I say? Carolyn is the lady with whom I share my Love, my life, my Self, my all. It is to this goddess I am blessed to be married, and to her that I dedicate this book. Carolyn, I Love you.

Contents

Acknowledgements / ix
Author's Note / xi
Introduction / xiii

ONE / 1

TWO / 11

THREE / 20

FOUR / 39

FIVE / 45

SIX / 54

SEVEN / 66

EIGHT / 79

NINE / 89

TEN / 97

ELEVEN / 112

TWELVE / 128

THIRTEEN / 141

FOURTEEN / 151

FIFTEEN / 164

SIXTEEN / 177

SEVENTEEN / 189

EIGHTEEN / 200

EPILOGUE / 219

ABOUT MICHAEL J. ROADS / 225

Acknowledgements

THE RIGHT PERSON is always there to either inspire me, or cajole me to keep writing. For me, Carolyn fills both roles. She inspires me by being who she is; a breath of Love and Light in my daily life. She cajoles me, sweet talks me, wheedles me, coaxes me, entices me and butters-me-up to either start writing, or keep on writing. All this, when I tell her that I have written my last book!

"I get emails, people are waiting for the next book." Or, "How can you not write another when people need it." And so on. Although I am not convinced by this, I have learned that resistance is futile!

Of course, I have perennial gratitude to the enigmatic Pan. Although it remains as inexplicable and completely unfathomable as to why our unique relationship continues, he offers an other-worldly and mystic reality for which I am very deeply grateful.

And then we have the cover photo. My dear friend Henry Watts spends hours with me each week, mostly working together in the Forest Garden, along with our third amigo, Bruno Streit. Henry loves photography and he excels at it. No matter how many times we have to move to the perfect location for every shot, Henry initiates it . . . and we move! Okay, I may grumble and groan a bit, but he always insists.

Henry is one of those few people that, when you meet them for the first time, it is like renewing an old acquaintance. Thank you,

Henry for the cover photo. Everybody who has seen it reckons you have perfectly caught the mischievous child/wise elder, me.

Then of course, we have the proof readers. Apart from the fact that I painstakingly and ruthlessly edit my own work, Carolyn is the first proof reader. If she says, "I don't like this, I think you should change it", it gets changed . . . mostly!

Next in line is Elisabeth Karsten. Because she is also an accomplished German author, to her any mistakes I make simply stand out . . . and she indicates them to me. It seems there is always a fair crop!

When Elisabeth began proof reading she was very ill. She asked if she could do it because she enjoys my books. She was able to read the complete manuscript before releasing the shadows of suffering, transitioning into the Love/Light of a greater metaphysical reality. Bon voyage, dearest Elisabeth. Thank you for the enrichment you brought into our lives.

At the same time, Sophie Marnez, who is French is going through much the same process. Of course, she is also fluent in English. Sophie is super-thorough, picking up all the conversational errors previously overlooked.

My final proof reader is Ankie van der Meer. Ankie is a Dutch lady who taught English, so her ability is very fine-tuned. She even finds overlooked errors in my 'published' books. Wow! What a team.

Thank you ladies for your work and dedication. You are all very dear friends and very deeply appreciated.

Also, thank you to my Japanese translator, Yasumi Okame. She is also my online organiser, and she has been my representative in Japan for over two decades. Yasumi refers to herself and all the above ladies as Michael's Angels. I agree . . . how blessed I am.

Lastly, but certainly not least, is my wonderful publisher, Denise Williams of Six Degrees Publishing Group in America. Despite the fact that we have never met, I feel that I know her. She is always ready for my next book, always happy with it, and forever helpful.

Thank you, Denise.

Author's Note

*I wish to be clear that the cover photo is not of Pan, but is a terracotta image of a forest gnome.
Also, this picture obviously depicts the physical me, not the metaphysical me!*

–Michael J. Roads

Introduction

This book is a blend of Pan... and me. Some of it is about my journeys into a tiny aspect of the mystery of that ninety-nine percent of life that has a frequency higher than our everyday physicality. This is the world that we never see; the world that doesn't exist for most people, yet it is there, mystical and mysterious. And, strangely, it is far more permanent than our brief physical lives that pass in a momentary flicker in the sheer, vast timelessness of eternal life.

Woven into this are a couple of flashbacks into my earlier metaphysical travels... where I considered it to be appropriate!

There was nothing easy about the early days of my meeting Pan. I may not have done it badly... but it could have been a lot better. I did not enter this relationship gracefully. I felt overwhelmed and threatened. My first meeting with Pan was when I was young enough to feel emotionally insecure... a condition I have happily grown beyond. Today I am fairly well known as a spiritual teacher. Maybe not world famous... yet... but my reputation is well established among seekers.

As with all modern day spiritual teachers, or so I assume,

I was not born into this vocation; it developed. Up to my early-thirties, I had no thoughts or feelings even remotely connected with spirituality, but despite this, the day arrived that changed my life. It began innocently enough at around 5:00 a.m. as I was walking from our house toward the milking shed on my dairy farm. My farm was based unsuitably—high production dairy farms are mostly on flat land—on the rugged foothills of Mt. Arthur, in Tasmania, the island state of Australia. As I walked past the small merry-go-round I had made for my children in the garden, I felt an impulse to jump on it and spin around. Unthinkingly, I did exactly that. Spinning around a few times, I was just beginning to wonder why I was wasting my time like this, when suddenly, out of the blue and with a massive shock wave to the very core of my Being, I was hit with a mighty strange and wondrous question: *who am I?*

This question shattered my life as I knew it. This was not an intellectual question born in my brain; it came out of nowhere, abruptly and powerfully, rising from some deep place within: who am I? It hit me so hard in my solar plexus that I folded over with a gasp, as though I had been kicked. And even more shocking . . . I did not know the answer!

Oh yes, I had a name, I had a family lineage. I had a wife and four children. I had friends . . . but . . . who I am, remained blank. This was not a question about the man or his name. Nor was it about the man and his many fearful and negative worries, or his deep anxieties due to feeling inadequate to the task of managing his farm in times of financial recession, a prolonged and brutal drought, and other hardships. This question was about the 'I' beyond the physical, who am 'I'? Beyond the physical me, where do 'I' come from? Where am 'I' going? I think you get the idea!

Looking back, I realise that when you *know that you don't know* you are in a good place. The worst place to be is when you *think that you do know*, but in reality, you do not. I was fortunate . . . in the moment of this universal question shattering my life, I strongly knew that I had no clue about myself or life. That was a shock in itself. Seriously, a couple of minutes prior to this, I really thought that I knew a lot about myself and life!

Shattering my life is no exaggeration. In that moment an obsession was birthed, abruptly and powerfully, deep in my psyche. As an Aries, I now realise it had to be that way, otherwise I would have dismissed it. I would like to borrow a cliché and describe the *who am I* question as a magnificent obsession, because in its own way it *was* magnificent, but it was also ruthless as it dismantled my old life and forced me to face all my fears. Truly, over the following couple of decades, to my current knowledge I was compelled to face *all* my fears.

Of course, in those days a younger me believed in fear. I had so many fears . . . what choice did I have? I had a long journey ahead to reach the place when I finally *experienced* that fear is not real. This is the place you reach when fear and you part company, because fear is the greatest and most powerful of all our illusions. Even though it is a toothless tiger, just contemplating life when you are over-burdened with anxieties is enough to make you quake with . . . fear! When we did part company, I thanked fear for all that it had taught me. I can tell you this, fear was not happy with our parting. It snarled at me, but when I laughed, it slunk away, fading as an old shadow caught, too late, in the strong morning sun.

I have often been asked how I defeated fear, but I did not defeat it; there is no defeating illusions because they were/are never real. I grew beyond fear to the place where *trust* is so powerful that anxiety, worries and fear no longer hold any power in your life.

Please take note: In this book I am no longer referring to travelling in my Light body. So many people have taken this so very literally they are lost in the image of a shapeless blob of Light. I am now making reference to travelling in my metaphysical body. And this body is anything other than a blob! The metaphysical body is larger and far more complex and refined than the physical, with far greater abilities that require a higher frequency in which to operate. This is our Truth. Add to this it is breathtakingly beautiful . . . and, dare I say, magnificent!!!

Also, please take note that once again I capitalise the first letter in all words that I wish to emphasise a more powerful and meaningful meaning! Love is the Power of Creation, while love is for apple pies. The same applies with Truth, which is universal, as compared with our personal truths. Equally, Change denotes far more than a change in the weather. Whole is perfect, rather than a whole rotten apple! As always, Oz is the land of Australia.

All my books—and this is the twenty-third—are based in my own spiritual or metaphysical experiences. Even if, to you, they seem a bit . . . *far out*. I can assure you that the world reality is far greater than we ever experience in our daily lives of illusion and delusion.

Universal reality is designed for sentient universal Beings. We are just one species of those sentient Beings, and we are certainly not at the top! For a very long time we have been held back, while also holding ourselves back! We are currently lost in the illusions of the intellect. We are lost in the erroneous concept that "Clever is God-like." In fact, clever holds hands with stupid. But hey . . . we have forever to get back on track.

My books are for those people who are <u>not</u> lost in their intellects; those people who live a more heart-based life. Interestingly, the seat of the intellect is in the brain, while the seat of intelligence is in the heart. Oh sure, not just the physical heart, but the powerful, all knowing, metaphysical heart.

Okay . . . so do we have a metaphysical brain as well, you might ask?

Actually, we do. But just as most people only use a small percentage of their brain, so most people live from only a tiny percentage of their heart's potential. We live lives of cleverness and separation, rather than lives of intelligence and connection . . . the One in All, the All in One. We mostly over-think and under-intuit everything.

As you might expect, over-thinking separates us from Truth, while under-intuiting does much the same. In other words, to evolve, we need to live far more from the heart while changing our relationship with our brain to a more holistic one.

This is why Change is sweeping through humanity. Real Change, not just a change of seasons!

I write my books to offer people a glimpse into a Greater Reality: a glimpse into the limitless vastness of all that IS. I offer people an opportunity to see that life is vastly different from the limited perspective of normal human beliefs.

Of course, this is not a book for all people. It is for the people of a more developed consciousness. These are not better people, or superior people, they are simply people who live a more heart-based life. Ah, yes, heart-based . . . and so the cycle continues!

Enjoy!

~ Michael J. Roads
Queensland, Oz

ONE

The Earth upon which your humanity abides is a kindergarten.

"IT NEVER ENDS, does it Pan?"
An inner chuckle. *It does not begin, either.*
"You're being evasive."
You are being vague.

I sigh. I am walking in my new Forest Garden. Actually, to call it a garden in this early stage of its development is probably being rather generous, but given another few years it will look like a garden, hopefully. Eventually, a magnificent one! Right now, after only a few months of creating it from cleared bushland, one needs a bit of imagination.

Pan, of course is not visibly with me, nor is he visible to me. For me, Pan *is* the Spirit of Nature. I long ago learned that Pan is not a Being in the way that we are Beings. Pan is a vast, conscious super-sentient energy of Love/intelligence, deeply connected with Nature on a universal scale. Literally, *the* Spirit of Nature. I have learned that Pan is not limited to our universe, but rather is an energy of the much greater multiverse. Pan is not singular in the way that Christians believe in a singular God—which probably means that I am no longer a Christian in the traditional sense. I really do not understand Pan intellectually; in fact, I am certain he is not understandable. It is enough for me that I am blessed by being tagged with his energy. Incidentally, when I write *his* or *he* this is technically inaccurate, but I am bound by the need to communicate with my readers, so I will continue in this vein.

My initial comment to Pan was a reflection on timelessness. Hence my shared observation, "It never ends." Let me be clear about this. As I walk in my Forest Garden, Pan has not made an appointment to be with me, or I with him. As I reflect, my thoughts are directed toward Pan and, with that tag, the consciousness that is Pan is ever present for me. There is nowhere in particular that Pan is, and equally, there is nowhere that Pan is not. Sorry if that seems crazy, but it makes perfect sense to me! Please, do not attempt to put Pan in a 'To be understood' box, because all you will eventually have is a seriously flawed and hugely inaccurate concept. I will share more about Pan—the enigmatic Spirit of Nature as I move into all this.

In truth, Pan is an inexplicable enigma . . . and I like it that way.

I continue our conversation. "I have no doubt you are correct."

Suppose I began to tell you things that are wrong. Would you just blindly believe and accept my words, or would you challenge them?

"Your energy would very subtly change, and I would know."

And do you think that I could not disguise such energy?

"I'm sure you could, but it would seem a pointless exercise."

Sitting on one of my log seats, I close my eyes. Sight and vision, along with thought, are very wonderful and powerful aspects of being human, but they can also be very distracting.

With my eyes closed to the beauty all around me, I *feel* into it. Nothing visual to stimulate, just the stimulation of listening and feeling. What is *feeling*, you might ask, and actually this is a good question. You are far more than your physical body. In fact, your body is the most dense aspect of you. It has a frequency slower than the speed of light, thus we can easily see it. However, occupying the same space as your physical body is a considerably larger metaphysical body of varying higher frequencies. This we cannot physically see.

This is the real you, the eternal metaphysical body of the soul you are. But equally, your physical body is also the body/vehicle of the soul you are. Both bodies are One in essence, simply resonating on different frequencies in the same space/moment.

It comes as a bit of a shock to consciously accept that of all the life around me in my forest garden, I can visually see less than one percent of it. This is where *extended feeling* comes into play. In that higher frequency body, we are able to feel/perceive/discern that which we cannot physically see. I admit, however, it does take rather a lot of practice!

I am aware that although physical eyes are seriously handicapped by being unable to see the higher frequencies, paradoxically, I am also that higher frequency body . . . as are you! I have learned that I can see with higher frequency non-physical eyes, and with a higher frequency perception. Most people are unaware of these higher abilities, so they are ignored, but they exist as a waiting potential for everyone. As a schoolboy I had the opportunity to learn to play the piano, but I never bothered to practice. I disliked it, so I did not learn, thus denying myself this wonderful ability for the rest of my life. However, as an adult I *have* bothered to learn to experience life and Nature from this higher frequency metaphysical body.

Nature has always been an important aspect of my life. As a boy, it was a place to hide away from aggressive adults.

On reflection, there was nothing special about me as a boy. I was just a regular kid, in and out of trouble, a bit lonely . . . but truly, I think most children are often lonely, even in the midst of their family. As adults, we learn how to handle our deep inner loneliness . . . or we don't. Probably, this is the more common scenario. Most adults have no idea that we live in a holistic world, that all life is One vast unified-field-of-energy expressing in a mind-boggling super-mega-multitude and diversity of physical forms. We look through our physical eyes and see separation. We see you and me: the tree and me: the dog and me: the car and me . . . and so on. It never seems to occur to us that the illusions of life are created and maintained by us; by our sheer inability to see much further than the end of our collective noses. Sadly, this creates a collective mass illusion, to which we all subscribe.

I smile fondly as I reflect back.

I think most of us who are happy with our life today would not change a thing in the past . . . even if we could. All the mischief and misadventures of my youth, plus the angry rebellion of my teen-age years, all add up to the experiences that influenced and guided me to be the person I am today . . . and I Love and embrace the wise and wonderful man I have grown into. No undue modesty here, no playing stupid games of self-love being ego-based, no need of agreement from others. I am who I am, and I can very happily live with this!

Who I am today has a relationship with Pan! I mentioned that Pan is not a Being. For me, Pan truly is the Spirit of Nature, but thinking, saying and writing Pan is so much easier. As you well know, Pan basically means 'all encompassing,' so it is a very descriptive term for an energy that is all encompassing to a degree far beyond our human comprehension. I can assure you that the mythology of Pan is as false as those who wrote it.

We look at life through physical eyes. We can see and even marvel at the depth and breadth of our vision, although most people tend to see the view around themselves rather as though imprinted on a vast, flat movie-screen. I suspect that this depends on how conscious a person is during their daily life. When life becomes routine and a bit monotonous, it becomes a sedative to curiosity. This is when the flat movie-screen mentality takes over. The eyes and brain no longer fully engage the actual depth and breadth of the panorama that surrounds them.

My relationship with Nature requires that I see the physical panorama of the world immediately around me, but it also requires me to go beyond this into the view offered when I engage my metaphysical eyes. My previous book, *Entering the Secret World of Nature*, explains how you are able to do this, expanding on all the ways I know of that can deepen and enrich your own relationship with Nature. However, I know that I, too, have much more to learn on this never-ending journey.

Pan . . . and Me

This vast Mystery of life beyond our physical senses intrigues me. Just imagine, we see less than 1 percent of what is. What about the other 99 percent? Sitting in my Forest Garden I open my eyes and look at the physicality of it. There are many gum trees, a scattering of young shrubs, the soil is covered in fallen leaves and natural debris, with wild grasses abounding. And it all has a buoyant and vibrant energy.

"Pan . . . I accept that what you perceive as reality in this area is probably vastly different from what I see and perceive. Is it possible to show me more of . . . whatever?"

Mixael, do you see the world in a fallen leaf?[1]

Hmm. "I understand the concept, and I can *feel* the world in a flower, but as you well know, I am seriously challenged to see the world in a fallen leaf."

Pick up any leaf and, closing your eyes, look through it to what is beyond.

I knew he would say something like this! "Pan, this is not easy for a limited human."

Then live within your limits or cease being so limited. Your choice.

With a sigh, I reach down to pick up a nearby leaf. It seems to be in a transition stage between retaining its leaf identity and becoming a piece of decaying organic cellulose.

Holding it in my fingers, I stare at it for a while, then close my eyes, hoping to see through it and beyond it.

Good . . . be with it.

I am aware that my humanness has quite a strong sense of linear time, while for Pan, this is non-existent. So, I settle down for the long haul!

As I bring my attention ever more fully to my task, my focus grows much more powerful. Stray thoughts flit and flutter in the brain like moths in the flickering light of a small candle, but I ignore them.

---

1. Although Michael is the name I was christened with, Mixael is my name as a walk-in. All this is explained further in the book.

It seems as though the world takes a deep in-breath, and I perceive decay spreading over the face of our planet Earth. It does not touch the physical world, seeming to hover like a faint mist of corruption, gathering and pooling in some areas while withdrawing from others. I am aware that it is most dense in the Northern hemisphere, yet dense is not the word. It is more as though it is clinging there, somehow concentrating in pools that are not physical, thus responding to completely different rules of movement and expression.

Gradually, I have no words for what I am seeing/perceiving. I feel rather troubled by what I perceive, but realise this is my own inner reaction. It is as though the decaying leaf has superimposed itself over the whole world, and I cannot find a space where the world is not showing any signs of decay at all.

Finally . . . all is leaf, slowly decaying as its life energies leach away.

* * *

I have no idea when, or quite if it ends, but I am slowly coming from some deep place of unnatural decay. It occurs to me that if a leaf can decay, so also can a planet. I feel very uncomfortable with this.

Very gradually, I am back into my physical awareness, feeling rather disturbed.

"Any chance that you will explain the decay?"

Any chance that you will intuitively inner-know exactly what it means? After all, you know my rules of engagement. You trust your inner-knowing, allowing it to guide and communicate with you.

I smile. "This goes hand in hand with look and learn, but don't touch and meddle."

I feel Pan inner-smile. *This also.*

"Prior to this experience, I would have said it is impossible for a planet to decay, and deep down I wish this to be true, yet the reality is that planets do eventually decay, but surely not with life still on them. However, I accept that many other factors are also involved. What I saw was decay hovering over the planet, rather like a metaphysical decay. What disturbs me is that the metaphysical precedes the physical . . . suggesting that this could, in fact, be ushering in a disastrous time for our planet Earth. This surprises and rather disturbs me."

And why is that?

"It surprises me because I thought that although the kids could mess up the classroom, they could not destroy it. Yet if this metaphysical decay and corruption becomes manifest physically, then our beloved planet is in serious trouble."

In a sense, you are correct about the kids being unable to destroy the planet, but they are certainly capable of destroying all human ability to live on the planet as you know it.

"What do you mean, the planet as I know it?"

If you have the question, Mixael, you have the answer!

I sigh. Pan is incredibly exacting in all our interactions. I can take nothing for granted, nor flippantly dismiss anything. As a spiritual teacher I teach that if you have a question in your brain, you also have the answer in your heart. We are holistic Beings, so we cannot have a half of a whole, even though the intellect would, and does, deny this. Questions always arise in the brain, and usually in the left-brain hemisphere. My observations as a travelling spiritual teacher indicate that a whole-brain person has considerably fewer questions than a left-brain dominant person!

When I just asked Pan, "What do you mean, the planet as I know it," I am compelled to acknowledge that my left-brain asked the question and that my heart does indeed, hold the answer. I have often pondered this very human habit of externalising questions rather than internalising them and trusting our own intuitive/heart replies. We mostly externalise because we do *not* trust ourselves. Our parental upbringing, our whole education system from child to adult, and our modern Western society all reduce us by encouraging us to seek answers and knowledge from an outside source. We accept and believe this far more than we accept and believe in ourselves. This is so obvious in our society today. It deepens our inadequacy which, in turn, deepens our already deep-seated anxieties. This does not make us wrong or bad, but it does nourish the illusions of deceit and the deceit of illusions.

"Yes, Pan. I do have the answer to the question I asked."

I feel an inner chuckle. *Pray share it with me.*

I am aware that technically, Pan knows my thoughts and every nuance of my emotions, yet he insists that I share as though he does not.

"Okay... the planet as I know it is our familiar three-dimensional world where we believe that physicality rules. I am aware that in the manner a full deck of cards could feasibly be described as all occupying the same space, so also our familiar planet Earth is just one planet in the full deck... as a metaphor. With cards there are fifty-two, but in the case of planet Earth all occupying the same space, there are hundreds of them in my limited awareness. So, using another metaphor, the planet as I know it is just one shade of several hundred shades of the same colour. I agree, we can make our particular planet unliveable for us, but this will not affect the other planets within the overall holistic Oneness of the many Earth planets.

Very good... this is not common knowledge.

"True, but it is very deniable knowledge for the intellect that seeks to understand that which it cannot possibly experience. To add to this, each Earth planet has a different frequency to all of the others, thus they actually do all occupy the *very same space*... in the way a pack of cards cannot."

Good... so where does this bring us in relationship to the decaying leaf and your familiar world?

Hmm... now isn't that a good question!

"This is my supposition, something that emerges from my intuition rather than being based on any external knowledge. Yet, to be fully honest, I have a degree of external knowledge that mixes and mingles with the alchemy of intuition to produce the insight of what I consider to be my inner-knowing. Sorry, Pan, but I may just be a more complicated creature than I ever previously supposed myself to be!"

You have always been more than you ever supposed yourself to be.
I feel a glow of warmth at his words.

"I think that I can safely say that our planet Earth is saturated in the energy of humanity. It has not always been like this. We reached the first billion people around the turn of the 19th century, and since then our numbers have been rapidly escalating. Probably the 19th-century energy remained reasonably stable, but during the 20th century this changed. We reached a critical mass of people, whereby our energy affected Earth by destabilising her. Humanity literally attacked the planet, declaring Nature an agricultural enemy that had to be controlled. Chemical warfare was heralded in, gradually changing the face of agriculture in many damaging ways.

"Instead of being co-creators with Nature, we became a pestilence on Earth. We ripped out the lungs of the Earth in her sacred ancient forests, finishing the job by making the oceans toxic. We lost our connection not only with the planet Earth but also with our spiritual Self. We moved ever further away from the potential of One humanity as we became lost in the illusion of all life-forms being separate. While there are many individual exceptions, the mass of humanity became ever more self-critical, leading in turn to varying degrees of self-hate. Our Western religions offer false teachings, and people blindly follow toward hopelessness.

"Of course, I could talk for several days on the many ways in which we have reduced ourselves to the lost and sick humanity we are today. I know humanity is not bad or criminal, Pan . . . just spiritually lost and energetically sick. I suspect that the decay the leaf showed me is the metaphysical decay of humanity today. I am aware that we are in an Age of Change as humanity enters a battle to keep our very souls from long-term enslavement."

A good summary. And why do you think this is happening?

"I think it is largely because we have become a sleeping, subconscious species. We are designed to be a fully conscious species, with the potential to become super-conscious. Instead, we have slipped into the greatest addiction possible for humanity . . . the *known* path: the more-of-the-same path. The deceptive path of needing to understand. The path of the intellect. The path that leads people into separation, isolation, apathy . . . and fear. Now, that path of sameness holds humanity in a pattern of decay.

The path forward is the path of the *unknown*. The path that unfolds itself in the eternal moment. The path of Intelligence, of Trust. The Great Path of unconditional Love. All this has been unwittingly abandoned."

Remember what you teach, Mixael. Humanity is a child. The Earth upon which your humanity abides is a kindergarten. This is where children learn to grow up into the sentient species they are.

I sigh. "Yes, it's easy to overlook this. I often wonder why I ever came to this particular Earth at this particular time."

An inner chuckle. *And yet . . . here you are.*

Two

The point an event begins and concludes may be many millennia of linear time apart, but in spherical time they both occupy the same moment.

I AM OFTEN ASKED how my relationship with Pan actually began. To be honest, when it began in this lifetime it had been many incarnations since I last had any connection with his energy. To me, Pan was a myth, the Green Man, a fantasy, even if a rather nice one. It felt reasonable that some type of God might be somehow embodied in Nature, although the aspects of Pan as a shaggy, humanoid type with goat legs, horns, and a liking for chasing virgins among the waterlilies down by the riverside did not do much for me! All in all, the myths were a turn off. The Green Man felt right, but the others did not make sense. If Pan was a beast-like figure, why did virgins get attracted to the riverside knowing that he lurked there? Sorry, not interested in such rubbish; so in this current life I shied away from our early seriously disturbing connections, even though I had, apparently, invited it. I felt that somehow, it was a case of mistaken identity . . . mine!

However, the Pan that I eventually connected with was breathtakingly beautiful. Nothing like the myth, not even remotely. I learned that if your consciousness could not perceive the beauty within Self, then you would only see and experience the beast. It surprises me to this day that the 'me' back then had a high enough state of consciousness to experience the unworldly beauty that Pan manifested. Of course, the manifestation was never really Pan, simply a creation with which I was comfortable.

As the shock of our initial encounters wore off, so Pan began to strip from me all my emotional borders and boundaries. The story of our first meetings and this process is told in detail in my book, *Journey into Nature*. I desperately needed Pan as a stable reference point during this period as Pan became my beloved teacher. However, just as I became comfortable with his familiar metaphysical human-like Pan manifestation, so he began to slowly, withdraw it. Eventually, I was left with only his energy tag, and the continuing ability to easily communicate.

The lesson was that Pan is not a Being, physical or metaphysical. Pan is a vast consciousness with a particular alignment for Nature. As I so often say and write, Pan *is* the very Spirit of Nature. So it was that when, in this current incarnation, I was unexpectedly exposed to him, I felt incredibly threatened within my framework of low self-esteem and emotional insecurity. In my late-thirties, I was in the throes of chasing who am I . . . in an attempt to find out *who I am!* I was completely lost in the process as my old beliefs and ideals were being confronted and painfully stripped away, one by one. I had a lot of inner-growing to do! Interestingly, although I did my best to sever my every connection with Pan, he would not allow it to happen. To add to my confusion, I was also compelled from within my own heart to *actively seek* this connection that I rejected because it so terrified me.

My greatest fear lay in that Pan had made an error. How could a school dropout at fourteen years of age be of any use to an Intelligence so vast and powerful? I felt like a total impostor. Overwhelmed does not get close. Very slowly, I learned that we already had a connection from a time before this . . . whatever that meant! I also learned that Pan was not at all interested in cleverness, as such, but rather he *liked* my quality of deep inner simplicity. This, he told me, is the foundation of true intelligence.

Who was I to argue!

(As I wrote earlier, the further I attempt to explain Pan, the more complicated it becomes. Pan has no *likes or dislikes*. He is not even vaguely human, so for me to put human attributes to him adds more to the fantasy, than to the reality of my experience. The fact is he communicates with me on 'my' level, because I could not remotely comprehend his.)

Gradually, our relationship grew and developed and, I admit that I did, indeed, flourish. I unfolded like a flower caressed by the morning sun. I grew so comfortable with his energy that there came a time when I asked him if we had ever had a prior connection to this lifetime. He confirmed that, yes, we had. Naturally enough, I asked him if we could revisit this encounter.

This is the story of that earlier connection in a time before this. I have told this story in one of my earlier books, but because this book is about Pan and me, I decided to repeat it for up-to-date clarity.

* * *

"Pan, did I first meet up with you in another frame of reality?"

I inner-feel Pan smile. *I wondered if you would make the connection.*

"Well, you never do anything with me that is random chance, or without purpose. So I looked for the purpose behind these visits to what appear to be random frames of reality. Bizarre they may be, but they are not random or meaningless at all."

As I go through my process of leaving my physical body and entering a higher state, I engage the metaphysical folds of reality which seem to continue like fresh-breaking waves, when suddenly I emerge in a place that feels vaguely familiar in a very deep, locked away region of my psyche. This is certainly not a solid, physical reality; it is far more ethereal, more purely metaphysical.

"The metaphysical precedes the physical," I say wonderingly. "Is that what this place is? A place where our physical world reality is, or was, emerging from a greater metaphysical reality?"

Good . . . very astute.

As I gaze around in this frame of reality, I find that my feelings, perception, and intuition give me as much input as my eyes, probably more. I have said this in previous books, but in my metaphysical body my eyes are not like physical eyes. I can shut out vision by choosing not to see, and by choice I can see distance and close-up as one and the same. As a human, whether I am physical or metaphysical, the stimulus that enters my consciousness is in direct proportion to my awareness. We are all like this! When in my metaphysical body, the *aware* or *conscious* factor increases the stimulus enormously. So now, to compensate for the 'unknown' aspect of what I am experiencing, I am consciously being attentive and aware.

I see a number of misty, almost gaseous Beings floating over a field of pale blue, fern-like foliage. I move over to the ghost-like Beings hoping to learn why I am here, and what, if any, connection I have with them. They seem to be drifting over the field without any real sense of direction, yet I perceive their intelligence, even if it is without purpose. I realise immediately this cannot be; where there is intelligence, there is purpose. Reaching out, I attempt to touch one of the Beings, and although there is no physical substance, I make contact. The Being is formless, but not shapeless. I can see the suggestion of what might eventually be a clearly defined human body, and strangely, the arm that I touched is now holding me.

There are no fingers holding me, no hand, yet the arm-like appendage is holding me. It seems as though we are now joined. I feel mild surprise, but no alarm. This Being *feels* completely harmless, and as it turns toward me I *feel* its curiosity.

"What is happening here, Pan? This Being is holding me."
Tell me what you are feeling from the Being.
"More than anything, a mild, undeveloped curiosity."
Why do you say undeveloped?
"Because its curiosity has no specifics, no direction."
You are sure of that?
"I think so. But I do get the strangest feeling that this has

happened before. It's as though I am holding me, in a non-time. As though I have connected with a me that existed before I was aware of being metaphysically conceived."

That is a surprisingly accurate summary. The Being holding you has become part of you. It cannot let go or make such a choice. You have become metaphysically melded.

"Oh gosh! This doesn't sound good. Can I tear myself away?"

If you do, you will kill the Being.

"Oh, my God, what have I done?"

As the Being faces me, I can see the suggestion of eyes, of a mouth, even of ears and nose, but they are unformed, for this Being does not need them. It now slowly brings its face closer to mine, and although I back away as far as I can with my hand held by its arm, I do not wish to hurt it, so my range is limited. The Being's face flows into and over mine . . . and suddenly my whole experience changes.

All the previously brilliant white illumination of atmospheric Light has gone, and I am floating in a world of colour beyond name or reckoning. I can see and smell colour, I can taste and hear colour, and I am nourished by the colours of my experience. I have a Being near me whom I am holding, and although I have no idea how it got here or what it is, I know that it is intelligent. As I hold it, I feel, via osmosis, *knowing* moving into me, and I mildly marvel at such a wonder. This Being is from another reality, another world, and although physical is a concept I cannot grasp, I know that this Being is far less physical than it realises.

As, in turn, I experience the feelings and knowings of the ethereal Being, I am aware it is receiving my inner feelings and knowing in a like manner. I am aware that it is the ethereal Being who is instigating this, and I realise that although this is an early stage of non-physical human development, it is of a greater intelligence than I had previously realised. I had assumed these Beings to be lesser than the human development of today. Now I have an insight into just how much we have lost to attain our present relationship with life. Deep down I realise that things could have been very different. But I also acknowledge the perfection; it is as it is.

I suddenly have an insight of such clarity, I gasp. "This is where it began, isn't it? I cannot separate from this Being without killing it, nor will I do that. Yet, I cannot stay here, for my physical body will die if, metaphysically, I do not return. Therefore, Pan, I can only assume that you will intervene. How, I don't know, but something has to happen. And when you intervene, intuition tells me something is going to be forever changed. I feel sure that on a soul level this Being is a pre-emergent probability-me, and from this time a connection is going to be created that will, in some way, connect the emergent Being I am with the Spirit of Nature that is you, even as it expresses in this time long, long before the present me. Is this correct?"

You have it basically correct. Linear time and timelessness are uneasy companions, for each has its own reality. In a timeless realm you unintentionally meddled with a Being, even if you did not instigate it. In that infinite moment, such an impossible possibility forever changed a probability you. As you surmise, I will have to intervene, otherwise the 'fall-out' will be of a far greater consequence. However, as you should realise, this had already happened before we came here, thus the 'connection' you mention could only have happened in the way it did.

"I'm sorry, but you lost me toward the end of that. Did you say that this had already happened before we came here? That doesn't make sense. I've never been here before. This is definitely my first visit."

Of course this is your first visit. You are assuming that time is a straight line heading toward a distant future. Wrong. In a greater reality, all time occupies the same moment. You have given this the term 'spherical time.' Linear time travels through the frames of reality that you travelled through, thus creating endless waves and echoes if you choose to do this. In this way, at a future time you are able to witness an event of distant past, bearing in mind that only because the event happened were you able to go back and witness it. The point an event begins and concludes may be many millennia of linear time apart, but in spherical time they both occupy the same moment.

The strangest thing is happening. Both the ethereal Being and I are absorbing this information, and as it enters our combined awareness, it creates the event that is about to happen. I struggle to understand how something that has already happened could be in the formation of happening, but the ethereal Being has no trouble at all. Linear time is a concept it has not yet faced. I struggle with this because I am bound by my knowledge of linear time, while the Ethereal Being is free of any struggle. It is because of this that I cease all my resistance.

Within me, I feel a soundless explosion, an explosion without force or violence, but of great power. And the ethereal Being and I are no longer joined.

"What happened?"

You made it possible for me to intervene.

"How did I do that? Surely you could do whatever was necessary without any help from me? What did I do?"

You created the situation; you had to resolve it. All I did was add the extra power needed to undo the melding. Yet, in the way of life, despite undoing the melding, it happened, and you, the ethereal Being, and I in this time-line will always retain a unique connection in consciousness. Now you know.

"You mean . . . this is our origin?"

Yes, this is what I am saying.

"And the ethereal Being is somehow still connected to both of us in consciousness?"

Yes, the ethereal Being precipitated the connection between us. Remembering also that in a greater reality all is One.

Another insight. "You and I actually became more deeply connected when that power seemed to explode inside me. A sort of metaphysical fusion took place, on however minor a level. Am I right?"

You are basically correct.

"I wish I had known this when I was younger, so I need not have gone through those years of denial."

Easy acceptance was always an available choice, yet the denial and eventual acceptance made that inner-power far more your own power rather than unaware acceptance. And, of course, you created the timing to eventually know what you now know.

I can only go so far with intellectual understanding. After that, I have to allow a greater, yet more submerged part of my consciousness to arise; the aspect of Self that knows. This is what I now do, looking at the ethereal Being from my own metaphysical perception. I feel enriched and privileged by the metaphysical experience we have shared.

"It really surprises me that I could actually touch the ethereal Being. I thought my metaphysical fingers would go through it. Yet when I touched it I knew beyond all doubt that this was my metaphysical forerunner, so to speak."

I encourage 'look and learn,' rather than 'touch and meddle'!

His inner-smile is like being touched by Love.

* * *

You, the reader, will now understand what I mean when I refer to being *tagged* by the energy of Pan. This does not mean that Pan keeps an eye out for me . . . as it were, or that I am within his constant attention; far from it. It is simply an energetic tag that in some incomprehensible way maintains a remote, but welcome connection. Hmm . . . I am again aware that the more I attempt to explain this, the further I drift from . . . !

We look at life and the world from a human reference point, obviously. However, even this is not so straightforward and simple as it might seem. Humanity is not like a rose bush covered in flowers that are all in the same stage of evolution, all with the same shade of pink. In our reality, we, the buds of humanity are all growing on the One Earth, but amazingly diverse in our many shades of energetic human colour. It is all to do with focus. Our personal colour shade depends on whether we are conscious and aware, or spiritually disinterested in our life, maintaining a far more materialistic and acquisitive perspective.

If we are consciously involved in our own evolution of consciousness, then the colour of our personal human focus will reflect this. Equally, when we are physically living our lives only, we will have a far more limited relationship with life and the world. This is the illusion. When we transition from the physical body into a purely metaphysical one, we have the opportunity to experience a greater reality. At this stage our perspective on life and the world will be enlarged to the degree that our consciousness can comprehend. This endlessly repeated process can be described as the evolution of human consciousness.

Three

Focus is an energy that structures your reality. Focus builds and shapes direction. Without a true focus, you hold away the essential energy of inner connection and its subsequent growth.

SITTING, RELAXING in my comfortable study, I gaze out of the window. After a while my eyes wander the small room. This is the room where I write my books, twenty-two to date. If you meditate in the same room on a regular basis, the room will take on the quiet, tranquil energy of meditation. It is the same in my study with writing. When I sit here with no vested things to say, or clever words to write, but simply open to life and inspiration, my energy seems to merge with mind and life until I am engaged. Sometimes nothing comes, just an unhurried blank. Then it is time for me to leave the study and engage the garden . . . which is of equal joy. I tend not to believe in writers block. This is when a person attempts to intellectually write something they have not yet energetically engaged.

My thoughts and focus turn toward the ancient forests that we have lost from our Earth. Closing my eyes, I physically relax, turning my attention toward the higher frequency body that we all have. This is the metaphysical body, although soul-body would be equally valid. There is a principle that guides humanity: *where you focus energy flows, and connects, and creates.* With my attention on the ancient forests, and my focus moving into the metaphysical, I am able to release the physical attachments and . . . I step between realities.

*   *   *

I am in a forest. As though in a vast cathedral of fantasy, immense trees covered in epiphytes cast the forest into a gloom; not a gloom in energy, but in a sheltering shade from a blazing sun. I am standing close to the trunk of one such giant tree.

I have no idea where I am. I choose not to make an intellectual choice of destination, thus I seldom plan a metaphysical journey, preferring the focus, the moment, and the energy to make the choice for me. This is not so much based in trust, as in not having a clue where to go! But, I do trust. This is why the method seems to work well for me. On one aspect I am fairly certain, the energy I am now feeling is not the energy of our current linear time.

"Pan, I'm puzzled. I feel your energy in this forest far more powerfully than in the forests of our time." I pause. "Okay, as I begin to formulate the question, so I am aware of the answer. It is not that you spend more time here than anywhere else, that is ridiculous. I am feeling that it is energetically obvious that in this period there are not almost eight billion people on the planet smothering Nature in a turmoil of imbalanced human energy."

As I so often tell you. Look and learn, be with it.

"But do not touch and meddle."

Exactly. Do you have a direct reason for being here, beyond that of which I am aware? Or is this a curiosity excursion?

I long ago learned that Pan reads my energy like a book; a very open book! I am unable to deceive him. Nor indeed, do I wish to. To Pan, I am transparent. He asks me a question like this for me to clarify my intent for myself. A procedure that is often required. As now, for example!

"You are correct. Curiosity brought me here, but also a longing to connect with ancient, old growth forest. We call this *old growth* because there is not much left, but in whatever time this is, it seems that it is still old growth forest.

"I can easily feel the energy of Nature spirits, far more so than when metaphysical in my own linear timeframe. I have a feeling that our current times in humanity affect our world in ways that are not immediately obvious. For example, I suspect that the many elementals of this forest are rather different from the forest elementals of my time."

The immense trees both in size and energy intrigue me.

"I would also like to connect with the tree elementals of this place and time in the world's history."

Be my guest.

I sigh. Sometimes Pan's sense of humour . . . !

"Would it help if you told me the when and where I am in history?"

Quite probably . . . but it will stretch you more if you engage the moment and release the when and where. They will be apparent if required.

"So will I be alone?"

If All is One, how does 'alone' have any reality? However, you are now perfectly capable of continuing your education without my further assistance.

I am alone.

I chuckle to myself. Pan's sheer sagacity in moments like this used to really aggravate me, but now it tickles my humour.

Time to be involved.

As, in my metaphysical body I move over to the nearest giant tree, I get the distinct impression of a natural cathedral in growth. It occurs to me that if true holy men, or those of special spiritual qualities felt the towering, grace-filled energy of trees like this . . . it may well have inspired them toward the architecture of the unnecessarily huge cathedrals with which we are familiar today. I mean, just how much space do you need above your head? I walk/float around the base of the tree, feeling its majestic energy. At what size or age does a tree grow from being a . . . a tree, to becoming a towering monument of Nature? This giant tree reminds me of a living shrine bearing witness to the miracle of the forest in which it grows.

As I move around the huge physical tree, I become aware that the metaphysical tree is vast beyond all normal measure. They all are in this forest. I am fully within the metaphysical body of the tree, and I have been since the moment I arrived. Just as a child takes time to develop movement in its limbs, to the eventual standing upright, and the first steps . . . so it is taking me timeless moments to orient myself to this vast, oh so energetically different tree, in this metaphysical reality.

It appears as though I am standing within a waterfall, but rather than water, it is flowing energy in which I stand in awe and wonder. Surely, the gods play with me! I have metaphysically entered many trees, experiencing their varying energies, but nothing that precedes this has prepared me for energy of this magnitude. Even as I reflect on it, like a blazing sun, insight reveals why it is like this. Clarity and certainty are twin streams of energy that are not so common in our present times, but within the sacred metaphysical embrace of this mighty and majestic tree, I *inner-know* that it is growing in a time long prior to our current human dominance.

I feel that humanity is alive in this distant time, but expressing a very different energy. As this *inner-knowing* blossoms, I am surprised as it reveals that although we have now multiplied into great numbers, we are not a thriving species by comparison with the overall harmony of this time.

Humanity is not a numbers or domination game. Are we perhaps unwittingly following in the footsteps of lemmings, despite our so-called cleverness? I am aware that in our current time our human consciousness is having a very substantial negative impact on Nature, but here, in this bygone age, all is held in the thrall of *natural balance*.

My insight continues to deepen. In our current times natural balance is lost, even in the most remote areas of wilderness. The consciousness of humanity leaves its taint in a way that is uniquely negative, and negatively unique! This is not to say that it is bad, or wrong . . . it is as it is, but it did not have to be this way.

I would like to think that as we go through our current pandemic of fear, there will be many people who will step beyond the veils of illusion. No doubt there will be those who cling and those who are able to let go. I am sure it has always been similar to this as a Great Cycle comes to its end, for it is also a time of resolution for all our personal inner conflicts.

As my perspective becomes more oriented within the metaphysical energy of the colossal tree, I realise rather than a waterfall of energy, it is a huge, slowly swirling vortex. It seems as though during my arrival I somehow stood within the vortex, but was untouched by it. This is changing. Very slowly and *gently*, as though I am deemed fragile, the vortex is passing *through* me. At first, I feel overheated, overwhelmed in what feels like heat exhaustion, and I am very uncomfortable. This is extremely unusual in my metaphysical body. However, even as the heat distress registers within me, I begin to feel cooler, like a refreshing breeze moving within.

In this breeze, inaudible words are carried, but even though I do not understand them, the breeze itself carries communication: *We are sorry for those moments of distress.*

By now I am cool and comfortable, feeling somehow lighter in spirit, lighter in energy, more buoyant. I smile, reassured.

We needed to raise your frequency to synthesise with us.

"Truly," I ask. "Am I so dense and heavy from my linear time?"

I inner-feel uplifting lightness. *Truly, humanity has a more dense energy in your time than of ours, but your metaphysical potential is far greater. You are rare inasmuch you are exploring that potential.*

"I probably am rare, but I am by no means alone in this. One of our big problems is that humanity believes itself to be a physical species. Many give lip service to their spirituality, but it is the few that actually explore and fully immerse themselves in it. Many others are hindered by ages of religious conditioning, not aware of the falsity of it. However, as an eternal species, this too will pass as we move slowly toward our destiny. I occasionally despair, but I should not. We have forever."

During this silent conversation I have been feeling what I can only describe as tendrils of inquiry moving within my consciousness. It actually feels very pleasant, rather like cool kisses on the inside!

"I take it that you are reading my energy?"

Correct. We are probing your intent . . . and finding none. No wants. In a human, this is very surprising. You are very open to the moment of being.

"I do have a focus, even if not a want."

Again, I feel uplifting lightness. *Focus relates to direction. Wants are based in attachments. Without focus you are a stray leaf withering in any wind that catches you.*

"Why withering?"

Because focus is an energy that structures your reality. Focus builds and shapes direction. Without focus, you hold away the essential energy of inner-connection and its subsequent growth.

"Hmm . . . I have never looked at it that way before. I am curious, how do you know so much about humanity?"

Since when has humanity been separate from the All?

The quality of the reply resonates deeply within, opening further insight. I know that these ancient trees were needed and necessary for human balance . . . we lost that as we destroyed them. It is only in this moment as I connect with the immense energy of this tree that I more fully comprehend that living for more than a thousand years builds up an incredible reservoir of conscious intelligence. Humanity believes that intelligence is the preserve of the human brain, but I have long seen past that intellectual error. Consciousness and intelligence go hand-in-hand. Animals are far more conscious-in-the-moment than people, and we see ample evidence of Intelligence in their abilities and capabilities.

"It seems that in the development of the human intellect, we have strayed far from intelligence. A species that destroys its own environment is a good example of this. Has this stupidity already begun in the people of this time?"

No, these humans are more consciously involved with Nature.

We are aware that the humanity of your time has lost this natural connection. You have much to relearn about humanity and much nonsense to abandon.

"I'm not sure that I really understand your last remark. What sort of nonsense?"

In your time humans worship what is termed as knowledge. We term much of that so-called knowledge as nonsense. It is false, based in beliefs that are narrow-minded because of your addiction to separation and linear time. Humanity has existed in various humanoid forms for millions of years. You are relatively new to Earth in your current form, but humanity has been associated with Earth for many millions of years . . . as it has with many other planets in this solar system.

"This deeply thrills me, for metaphysically I have seen evidence of this, although I was unsure if I could accept my experience as real and unbiased. I am certain that on this Earth we have lived in times of tiny, almost elf-like humans as well as the towering giants that I have experienced."

When I am being energetically uplifted in the way that I now am, it enables me to synthesise not only with this remarkable tree, but also the forest as a whole. I feel it igniting insights and intuition. As a new insight forms, I communicate it to the tree.

"It is obvious to me that our current humanity is on a decline with regards to intelligence. For example, so much of our clever electronic technology is destructive to us. Even though it makes our lifestyles easier, its disruptive energy makes us sick. There is ample evidence of this available to all people, but it is mostly ignored. Humanity has adopted a head-in-the-sand approach, although I have to say there are many exceptions; people who do use this technology with great caution. Add to this our pathological destruction of our global environment and it becomes obvious that as a species we have subconsciously disconnected from intelligence.

"In our era of a depleted Nature, along with our disconnection from Nature, we have created a situation where it is increasingly difficult to fully integrate with conscious intelligence. This, plus our subconscious addiction to the intellect means that we are seldom fully conscious; certainly not as a species, and only comparatively few as individuals. Intelligence requires us to be fully conscious. This is now rare. Our intellects have become our substitute, filled with knowledge based in fear, isolation, separation; this in turn spawns blame, anger and retribution . . . on and on."

Just as you translate our communication energy into words for you to understand, so we translate your words back into communication energy for us to comprehend. We resonate with what you say, but you have little idea of how understated your insight is into a reduced and limited Nature with regard to human intelligence. To see in the dark you require light. To fully integrate with intelligence, Nature IS your light. Humanity of your time has so greatly reduced the power of that light, it is but a glimmer. Thus it is that humanity is no more than a glimmer of its greater potential.

I stand motionless in shock.

It is not the words that shock me, it is the flood of insight into just what our potential could have been had we taken a different path. We are truly thousands of years behind our greater potential. As crazy as it seems, our unwise path was the agricultural one; along with the ownership of land. Once we believed that we could *own* land, we began to change our whole relationship with Nature, with the Earth and with each other. How stupid. We cannot own land. Nobody can. Long after our family name is forgotten, the land is still there, still unowned. As ownership was born, so fear, avarice and greed were given birth. I am reminded of the ongoing conflict between Israel and Palestine as they constantly quarrel and fight over the Gaza Strip. Small conflicts escalate into big wars. Foolish and misguided, we are as we are, but our fears and negativity did not lead us to our greater potential . . . which still awaits.

I speak to the tree of wisdom once more.

"How aware of me are you?"

You already know the answer to your question. As our tendrils of energy probe your energetic body, so all of you is known to us. Linear time is of no consequence. Your whole-of-life-experience physically and metaphysically is revealed to us. We knew we had your permission.

I chuckle. "Yes. It is no good being a metaphysical traveller if you have a hidden agenda . . . or secrets!"

Waves of refreshing uplifting energy sweep through me. Very pleasant. I like to think this is Nature's, or the trees', equivalent of chuckling.

"So you know all about my journey into a potential future which is a happening-now time, where the people are nomadic? Those people are conscious and very connected to Nature and intelligence.

Yes, we know of this era. This nomadic time is as much the now for us as your linear time, or this seemingly long, long ago time you are visiting. Metaphysically, all is One. Linear time is but a purposeful illusion.

I should perhaps explain that I describe the time of a greater reality as spherical time: all time occupies the same moment. As is clear and apparent to everyone, physically we live in linear time. What is seldom realised is that metaphysically we live in spherical time. In effect, this means that we live in two time zones simultaneously. Illusions are held in linear time, while Truth is found in spherical time. There are many futures which are happening now in spherical time, each offering their own speciality regarding energy, learning and conscious growth.

This is where we are at, now. By our own choice in the way we think and live, we either continue on the current timeline, or we shift into one of the new spherical timelines that take us into a new future. The future-now I mentioned is where nomadic people of a considerably higher consciousness are living. A future now is a linear concept, while in a greater reality it occupies this moment in spherical time. I wrote about this in my book, *Stepping . . . Between . . . Realities*.

I find it appropriate to offer it again here.

To explain: I am exploring consciousness in one of the many levels of the astral worlds of Nature. I have just been lured into a waterfall, which then deposits me into the World River.

* * *

"Where do you come from? Where do you flow to? I ask."

From and to are meaningful in the physical world, but when you are One with the energy of many worlds, your question becomes meaningless. Flowing is Beingness. This is considered to be a world of land by land dwellers, but with its great percentage as water, it is truly a water world.

I struggle to remember. "We have a drought where I live . . . in a water world?"

Drought is not the absence of water; drought is the absence of energy flow. Humans do nothing but interfere with flow, rarely facilitating it. Want impedes flow. Human greed interferes with flow. Human corruption interferes with flow. Control interferes with flow. Ripping open the skin of the Earth interferes with flow. Destroying the forests interferes with flow. Polluting the rivers and oceans interferes with flow. Killing each other . . .

"Okay, okay . . . I get your meaning."

Where your people live . . . ownership of a place interferes with flow. If your humanity was nomadic, you would all grow in consciousness at a greatly accelerated speed. Nothing to own, to possess, to get attached to . . . all these interfere with flow.

"Many people have no homes . . . neither do they have flow."

Child, they lost flow long, long before they lost their homes. Losing flow is why they lost, and are losing, their homes. Do you not see this?

"Yes, I accept your wisdom . . . but humanity will never again be nomadic."

Wrong. Certain reality frames of wiser, more advanced humans are entirely nomadic, as many of your people will be in the not too distant future. Your human way is working against you, not with you. Nomadic does not suggest more primitive. It is fluid and flowing, rather than fixed and stuck.

"I agree. The idea of a nomadic life holds much appeal. What a relationship with the natural world it would be."

Exactly. No cities compacting the soil, few industries, but a flow with Nature where all your needs are naturally met, rather than needs and wants created, and then destructively manufactured or worked for.

"You create a vision for humanity I have never even imagined. I confess, I love my home among the gum trees, but to be free in the way you describe would be even more wonderful."

As she communicates with me, the World River touches energies in me, creating inner vision and revelation that is neither mental nor emotional. Some sensory energy that is more basic, yet is far more evolved, and involved, than any of the normal senses we use for daily living. I cannot explain, but she opens the metaphysical-me to a newness beyond any human newness I have experienced. And yes, I feel her energy as feminine!

Within the energy current of the World River I see/experience/perceive/connect-with a humanity moving in large families, or tribes, over the face of the Earth. These are a refined and beautiful people, exuding vibrant health and energy. Their relationship with Nature is far beyond anything of our current humanity. I watch a large family of maybe two to three hundred people, who are following a wide highway through a temperate forest. This highway is not designed for mechanical traffic. It is for humans, and whatever wild animals might care to use it. These highways are not made by people, nor are they permanent; they are created by Nature to conform with natural law. This one appears to be compacted soil, yet when it rains there is never any mud. Equally, if the hot sun beats onto a highway on the open plains, there is no dust. Every few years the highways disappear as the forest, scrub, or plains grass swiftly re-grow over them, while new highways re-form close by. When a highway is being created by cooperating with the great devas of the Earth and Nature, it is as though the Earth moves itself, taking trees, boulders, or any other obstacles with it, and all the vegetation continues growing undisturbed. Thus the basic highways are created. In this frame of reality, what we consider as miracles are a daily and commonplace occurrence.

As I watch this large family group travelling through the forest, they stop for the night. They have transport without wheels. Transport that seems to simply float, silently and efficiently, with no size limit. Futuristic homes travel/float with them, looking rather like house-sized, flat-based, opaque bubbles. I have no idea how the technology works, but it is obvious that these people have mastered the use of anti-gravity. Wherever they stop, there is always waiting an abundance of trees laden with fruit for these vegetarian people to eat. There is no farming of the land; the land willingly gives forth its bounty, and this bounty is always available.

They live in cooperation with all the Beings and energies of Nature, and the offering of the people is one that honours a sacred trust. They bless the food they eat, they bless the land on which they travel, they honour the whole planet with a benign dominion. These are not a people who drop a casual "Thank you". They live their Love and regard for Nature. Nothing is exploited. Nothing is wasted. The people maintain an aspect of themselves that holds an awareness of the Nature that surrounds them, and even while in laughing conversation they maintain this natural, easy vigilance. They are consciously connected to their physical world and its environment, but more importantly, they are connected to the holistic spiritual world, embracing its spiritual environment. For them, they and their environment are One.

The old cities of the Earth do not exist here. The numbers of people living on the planet are in complete harmony with the Earth's capacity to feed and nurture them. Many people of a higher consciousness have moved to other outlying planets that support life. They, too, live at One with their home-world. Humanity has learned a different way to live, a different way of being; they have found the Way of Balance. Sickness and illness are almost obsolete. Lives are considerably longer. Harmony has become the genetic pattern of a more whole and efficient human DNA, and each physical body reflects this change. I am aware that all this I am experiencing is to do with the humanity of a higher consciousness. Those of a lower consciousness are still involved in creating their daily struggle. This is not bad, nor is it a punishment. The lesson is that we are creating ourselves as eternal Beings, and that we are all far from finished!

However, above and beyond all these amazing changes, humans are no longer alone on the planet—and they have learned that they never were. Yes, there are quite a few visiting Beings from other worlds, studying the marvellous symbiosis that the people of Earth have with their planet, and with Nature. But above and beyond this are the natural denizens of Nature that do not have a human physicality. The people live with a joyful awareness and in a meaningful relationship with the many and varied devas, and the throngs of the mystical elementals and spirits of Nature.

This family group is gathered around the fruiting trees and shrubs, picking and eating and blessing. These fruit trees and shrubs will always be bearing fruit when a family or tribe arrives with need of nourishment. Their production is no longer linked to seasons and weather, but linked instead to human need and the common, sacred bond they share. It is the same with water, with natural springs bubbling out of the ground wherever they are needed. These food/water stations could be likened to higher consciousness service stations for cars on our own highways. Naturally enough, these people also carry food and water. As I watch, I see a vast, devic Being of pure Love/Light energy containing the whole family group and much of the forest in their area. I am hugely surprised, however, as I watch the Love/Light dissolve into a number of Love/Light Beings - devas - all interacting with the human family. They connect in telepathic communication, even holding hands and occasionally embracing during these profound moments.

"What I see is so wonderful . . . is this our future?"

It is 'a' future, one of many probabilities. For the people you are observing, it is their current life on Earth. This is real; it is happening. They have a consciousness at One with the All, yet they are individuals of a higher order of individuality than your people have presently attained. For many people of your time, this is their probable future, for others, *their path of consciousness will take different directions. It seems so difficult for your people to grasp that they are the absolute creators of their lives; their past, present, and future. Not the creators of their spiritual essence, but of the lives they live.*

"This is what I teach. As insufficient as it may be, I give it my all."

When you give your all, you touch into a higher order. Give it no thought, but know that it touches and ignites an order of magnitude far beyond the endeavours of a single person.

The words of the World River touch me with a deep inner reassurance I was not aware of needing.

As I observe this nomadic family, I become aware of many more of these large family groups, and also numerous other groups travelling the world. Everywhere they travel it is with the cooperation of a revered Nature. The scene changes and I see various groups converging at what appears to be a huge seaport. Here, indeed, there are very large, permanent, futuristic buildings. However, even these permanent installations have only the lightest contact with the Earth. Made with some super-tough, lightweight substance, a few enormous pylons with incredible, bird-like, widespread feet, hold the buildings which hang suspended in huge, web-like nets of some gossamer-thin substance. It all has a vaguely spider's web appearance, yet is both massive and stunningly beautiful in the overall flow and curvature. I am grateful that my observations are accompanied by an inner-knowing of what I am seeing . . . courtesy of the World River.

There is no air flight. Not because this is impossible; it is a choice. Nobody is in a hurry. The world of hurry, hurry, hurry does not exist here. Travelling across the world, from one country to another, is by ocean transport. Countries are no longer owned; no passports are required. People can travel whenever, and to wherever they choose. Equally, they can live wherever they wish. Just as transport on the land hovers, so also it hovers on the seas and oceans. The ships are wide, huge, and very comfortable. They have similar shipping lanes to us, but the behaviour of the weather and the oceans in these many shipping lanes, is always calm. The devas of the oceans and the devas of the winds cooperate with the humans for the benefit of all. Naturally, the oceans are pure, filled with a vast array of sea life, while whales, dolphins and marine mammals abound.

I am thrilled to see that a new order of intelligence is rapidly arising in the oceans. With the encouragement, guidance, and assistance of humanity, the large octopi are making a great, quantum leap in consciousness. The awareness of the many other octopus species is growing swiftly under the stimulus of their own unique, alien intelligence. Many people have established community homes in the oceans. Some have moderated their bodies to breathe oxygen from the water; other, less permanent or visiting people, use small, unobtrusive, artificial breathing devices. The people who have moderated their bodies have chosen to spend most of their lives guiding and inspiring the larger octopi species in their evolution. They have already created a complex, yet reasonably complete light, colour, sound- vibrations communication system between their two species, despite their utterly different environments and totally different concepts on the nature of reality.

I watch a hovering, sea-going vessel crossing an ocean. It is not as tall as our largest are today, but it is much wider, more stable. Wide enough to comfortably hold a village. The— at a guess—few thousand people who are being transported live in rooms the equivalent size of ones in our better hotels. There are no upper or lower classes, no richer or poorer, in fact, no currency other than goodwill and blessings. I need to re-emphasise that blessings are not a few muttered words of prayer. Blessings are a focus of such intensity of the Light from one person to another, or to wherever it is directed, be it Nature, the devas, whatever— that the person, or Nature, or whatever is being blessed, actually glows with a soft illumination. Blessings are a very powerful gift of high impact, strongly focused Love energy. They are a soul gift, healing, harmonising, and extremely beneficial. They are literally, a hallowed, very sacred act.

As I watch this crossing, I see that the ocean, no matter how rough or stormy it may be, becomes calm as the oceanic vessel approaches, while the wind drops to a breeze. With their passing, the weather and ocean return to their original pattern. No rough passage here! This level of cooperation is literally awesome; a demonstration of what can be achieved by honouring and acknowledging the great devas of water and wind!

The World River now switches my view/connection/experience to what I can only describe as a huge community city. The one I am watching is located in a desert, but I learn that others exist in forests, on the very high, permanent snow-fields, on lower mountains, some 'on' the oceans, a few 'under' the oceans, and several in other natural high-energy places. They appear as huge—and I mean huge—translucent domes that contain many thousands of smaller, non-permanent dome homes.

Each community city consists of a single huge, flat-based translucent and transparent dome. The top of the dome is translucent, allowing light to enter. I do not know how it is done, but this natural light is even empowered or enhanced, in dull and cloudy weather. For about twenty metres in height the sides of the dome are startlingly transparent, giving the visual effect of the translucent top seeming to float above the city. The dome reaches up to maybe one hundred metres high, and appears to be self-cleaning! I can only guess at the overall size, but I would say that the dome could hold a city of around one to two million people. The whole effect is very natural and organic; high-rise buildings and concrete do not exist here.

Looking through a dome into a community city reveals the visual effect of many shades of green, dotted with the many mobile translucent dome homes among all the gardens and vegetation. I should also mention that the dome homes are able to take on colours. How they do this I have no idea. The colours are subtle, a single dome home blending the colour/shades of spring, summer, autumn and winter that are natural in Nature. The effect is very harmonious and relaxing; visually it is quietly beautiful. Apparently, they can be permanent colour, or ever changing, or any combination!

Under the huge domes that contain the city, there are hundreds of thousands of fruiting trees, fruiting shrubs, and vegetable gardens of designs beyond description. They abound. All this living, ever-available food is for the people to help themselves. Under the city dome, it is literally a green oasis. All transport roads appear to be like golfing freeways, but they are not grass. They seem to be composed of a form of green/grey, lichen-type growth. Whatever it is, it is both durable and vibrant, and continually replacing itself. Their methods of transport range from hover-seats, to hover-everything you can image! Plus a large amount of easy, flowing, joyful, vibrant, willing walking! As with the homes of the nomadic groups, all the homes under the great dome hover. The pressure and impact on the soil is absolutely minimal. Nature rejoices in these community cities. I learn that the homes are not located permanently. When a family begins another journey, the home floats with them. The city is constantly emptying and filling in a flow of human energy; a flow which means the community city is constantly reshaping and recreating its interior design.

Everywhere I look I see the startling white colour of Balance. The reds of Chaos and blacks of Order seem to be non-existent or entirely positive. Balance is both the dynamic and the structure of life in our 3–D world! The World River tells me that even these cities can, and do, move their location every now and then, according to the needs of Nature. A few tens of kilometres of coordinated movement, and they settle again into another naturally prepared area and into another natural cycle of Nature. This is a humanity that places the needs of Nature before its own, and all prosper and thrive from this high and fine regard.

Focus now more on the Spirits of Nature. See what is possible when the energies of the physical and the spiritual are joyfully harnessed for the benefit of all.

My vision/connection changes on its own accord. I am still observing the community city. A community city; no other words can adequately describe it. Our cities thrive and grow on commerce, depending on such for their continuity, but not so in this reality. Here, the cities are vibrant, holistic communities—thriving on thriving people! Each person shares their creativity and passion for life with all people. I see what we call restaurants, but here, undercover, thus not needing roofs, they are built around multi-tiered community gardens of enormous diversity and complexity. These provide endless varieties of living, organic food from a fully cooperative soil. These areas also contain complex, multi-tiered water gardens, with a very large range of amazing, edible, aquatic plants. Some of these aquatic plants even fruit underwater! It is all an astonishing and very beautiful presentation.

Ah, now I see the Nature Spirits. These are a type I have never before seen, swarming like white bumblebees over all these multi-tiered gardens. I watch as they fly in and out of the leaves, branches, flowers and fruits of the gardens. With them, working in a coordinated pattern of movement, I see large numbers of earth-like Nature Spirits. Looking like clods of animated soil, they swarm through the earth as though utterly frantic, such is their inexhaustible energy. In the water gardens small, sylph-like Nature Spirits dance and flow with the constantly moving water in what, to casual sight, appear as flickering lights moving within and over the water. No frantic soil energy here, but a pace and cadence of flow and grace. And somehow, orchestrating all this, are tall, gnome-like Nature Beings who wander with clear purpose and intent throughout the entire, multi-tiered gardens. These Nature Beings are not performing any task other than holding a laser-like intent for all the Nature Spirits involved in the food production. I am aware that each of these Nature Spirits fits in with all the others in One, cohesive Whole. No energy is obsolete or wasted. Interestingly, there are many hundreds of these restaurants/gardens scattered throughout the whole city community.

Finally, over-lighting each restaurant/food garden, are the individual, deva energies which link and connect holistically with the vast and incredible over-lighting deva of the whole beautiful community/city. Utterly amazing! What a triumph of divine order—of complete, holistic cooperation.

"Thank you, World River, for showing me all this. What I have seen and experienced here feeds and nourishes a part of me that I now realise was hungry. I am truly grateful."

I, too, have been nourished. I have shared your experiences as you observed and marvelled at this holistic world reality. Feeling the newness in you has been a newness within me, for we are not separate. Feeling your wonder and awe has awoken in me something that slumbered, so I, too, am grateful. All that I have received will go into new creation, just as all you have received will gradually recreate your life . . . and with you, the lives of many others. Go in Love.

I cannot help but wonder at the convergence of the many realities I have visited over the years. Do they converge, or are they independent streams of consciousness flowing into a greater river of consciousness of which I know nothing?

Four

'You' are funny. Should you not have asked this question many years ago? But we like your honesty, your ability to be humble. You have met many metaphysical Beings. Some have a physical body through which to express, as you do, while others are completely metaphysical, having evolved beyond all need for a physical vehicle.

"Do you know of the World River?" I ask the huge tree.

As I ask the question, I feel as though the tree is consciously merging me with the whole forest of ancient trees. The energy is incredible, affecting me in a way I have not previously experienced. I feel as though I am within a giant tuning-fork, vibrating at a frequency far higher than is normal for me.

Yes, we are aware of that which you refer to as the World River. It is a flow of universal energy that spans worlds, solar systems and galaxies. All of Nature is held in the flow of the World River.

Wow . . . this is more than I expected. I knew that the World River is universal energy, for I once swam in it. I had expected water, but could you not describe an inexplicable liquid energy as some kind of water?

Metaphysically, I lift up into the air so that I am high above the forest. As far as I can see by wilfully using the range of physical eyes I see forest. I obviously have no physical body here, nor physical eyes, but by willing it I have the ability to see around me as I would through normal eyesight. I also have the ability to see far beyond normal eyesight, as though drawing that which I view toward me . . . a sort of far-sight! More and more I am learning that my metaphysical body is far more tuned-in and effective than my normal physical body. This is the case, of course, for everyone. Metaphysically, I am not stuck in a one way, two-eye focus only. I can see everything around me simultaneously simply by choosing to do so. On a soul level I am aware that this is also possible while in the physical body, but it would take a life of enormous dedication to bring these skills to the fore. And why would you need to when we already possess the metaphysical ability?

The simple reality is that in our intellectual modern world, most people would not believe what I am writing here of my metaphysical experiences. Most people are prisoners of their beliefs and their body. What is death but an opening of the prison doors? Until, in the next incarnation, people once again willingly imprison themselves!

I am in one of my favourite places, about a hundred metres above the ground sitting in the lotus position. I can select an area of forest and gaze into it closely. I can also magnify what I am focussing on. I am able to open up inner senses that I did not realise I had. Let me explain this: when communicating with that single ancient tree, all my other senses closed down so that my ability to concentrate and focus was undisturbed. I did not intend to do this, it simply happened because this is what was required . . . for me! Another person might have done it differently.

Now, fully engaging the forest as a vast, green ocean of leaves and biological diversity, I become aware of the shrill calls, whistles, shrieks and sounds of the overwhelming numbers of hidden animals, birds and insects. Despite this noisy attraction—distraction!—I endeavour to get some idea of the immensity of the actual forest. As I attempt this, I am overwhelmed by the sheer vastness of the forest. It seems to go on forever.

I have a sudden inner-knowing that I am in Gondwanaland, of many ages ago. This explains the incredible energy, the totally-without-human-taint energy that I am experiencing. Humans are here, but they are One with Nature and far more aware/conscious than us, even though they are without our present intellectual development. This is yet to come . . . and at what a terrible price!

With a sigh, I float down to the forest, intending to simply walk beneath these god-like trees that no longer exist in my time. A thousand plus years of tree growth creates a field of energy that has no human description. And to be in a forest where millions of trees, most over a thousand years of growth cover the land, it truly does defy depiction or explanation.

Many birds are here, flying among the vast, interwoven maze of differing branches while completely unaware of me. I wonder if I was physical if they would continue to be unafraid.

If you were physical in your body of the Earth time you physically live in, your energy could be similar to a destructive typhoon moving through this forest. Luckily, this cannot happen.

I stop, dumbfounded. I am aware that the forest as a Whole has just communicated with me, but the content is seriously demoralising.

"Why? Is my energy so heavy, so very different or dangerous on a physical level?"

This is not a matter of judgement, nor is it personal. You have an energy-field which is relevant to your current time of Earth. Your modern Earth energy-field and this forest energy-field are aeons apart. It would be almost like comparing the sun with the moon. Of course, this is deliberately exaggerated, but only in order for you to realise that the difference is huge.

"And yet . . . this difference cannot even be seen."

By your 'eyes' maybe, but as a metaphysical Being you are very moved by the 'difference' in this energy to any that you have previously experienced.

I nod. "You are right. As I look at the trees, I am focussing on the physical similarity, but energetically, this time and mine are more than worlds apart. And yet . . . how does linear time and spherical time deal with this?"

As you know, linear time is part of the illusion. It keeps your focus in the physical world, where the many expressions of Nature demonstrate the passing of linear time. But you are not truly a physical Being. So by being here metaphysically, are you in the distant past, or is this an aspect of all time occupying the same moment? Is this a conundrum for you, or is it obvious?

"Hmm . . . at the risk of being completely wrong, why does it have to be one or the other? It seems to me that both are true. I am here in the now, which is now in the wholeness of all time, both linear and spherical."

I feel an inner energy as though a wave of humour is rippling through me. I guess it's an inner-smile . . . somehow different, but the same.

We are pleased that you did not make the choice of separation. People of your time seldom see the connections. Everything must be separated and isolated so it can be intellectually analysed.

"Sadly, this is our flawed educational system. Because it is based in illusion, it has no choice but to basically teach through the false beliefs of separation and isolation. This is so deeply embedded in us that many of our elderly die of sheer loneliness within the isolation of their reality, although I doubt if this is ever written as a cause of death." I pause, my thoughts moving in a new direction.

"As the vast and ancient forest you are, I am aware that I have no idea of the depth and breadth of your knowing. I accept that our telepathic communication translates into me in my own words, and that it triggers sudden insights, and deep intuitive leaps . . . these all go with conscious telepathy. Despite this, I am aware of basically being intellectual when physical, as my education taught me to be reasonably knowledgeable. When metaphysical I am less mental and intellectual and far more based in 'directly knowing,' which is a very different cognitive ability."

I sigh. "I am having trouble wording my question. Physically, I have a brain and a heart. Physically, you, as a forest, do not have a physical brain or heart. I am struggling to fully comprehend how we can be having this conversation. This, after having spent much of this life able to communicate with Nature! What is the actual dynamics of our communication? How is it possible?"

Once again I feel that ripple of humour energy. How can a forest have a sense of humour? Pan, yes . . . but a forest? And what is funny?

'You' are funny. Should you not have asked this question many years ago? But we like your honesty, your ability to be humble. You have met many metaphysical Beings. Some have a physical body through which to express, as you do, while others are completely metaphysical, having evolved beyond all need for a physical vehicle. Those purely metaphysical Beings have no physical brain or heart, yet they have an intelligence that is far greater than humanity of your time-frame. Of course, we acknowledge that there are almost countless humans of a more advanced intelligence who have also evolved beyond the need of a physical body.

As you communicate with this forest, you are communicating with a Being that expresses through the Whole Forest. You would call this Being a deva. I, as the deva, speak as we, the forest, for this is my overall expression. As a Being I have evolved beyond the need of a physical heart and brain. I am sorry, but these are organs for reasonably primitive Beings. Intelligence is conscious energy, not needing any physical organ through which to express. It is universal, as I am. As you know, it is your heart which expresses intelligence, while your brain works at maintaining a sense of identity through your intellect. Do you seriously believe that intelligence and cognition need a physical body? 'Direct knowing,' as you call it, is a powerful direct cognitive connection with the All.

Throughout this strong reply to my question, I have felt a sense of mild shock and shame. Deeper within, I knew this. Why had I not allowed it to surface into my awareness? I know better than this, hence my shame.

Even though these were silent thoughts to myself, when with a Being of this calibre I might as well have screamed them aloud.

Hush child. Do not berate yourself. You live in a world of much lower consciousness. Not lower or lesser Beings, but young Beings, still in a junior state of development. In this collective energy we admire your ability to hold so much of yourself in a greater reality, rather than being completely lost in the illusions of personal and consensual realities.

"Thank you for your kindness. The energy of your communication has allowed me to stabilise my emotional wobble." I smile to myself. "I am not a man of many questions when I am focussed in physicality. I am strongly inclined toward a whole-brain way of living, thus I trust my intuition and deeper feelings. In people like me they are a very adequate and insightful form of communication with the world around us. Yet . . . when I am metaphysical with a Being of your magnitude, questions just seem to come bubbling to the surface. I beg your patience to answer just one . . . or maybe two more."

This time the ripple of humour energy is so strong, I am also chuckling. I know immediately that this is my permission to ask.

"Thank you. When I first arrived here in this ancient forest, I was with a vast, enormous tree. It has a field of energy that for me is beyond my intellectual ability to describe, and yet, deep down in my consciousness I felt a mysterious familiarity. I feel it now."

I am groping for adequate words. "This feeling of deep knowing, of connection is not new to me. I suspect that it is an ages old connection. If Beings evolve in consciousness . . . and in my awareness, they do, then why am I growing away from this connection with the All, instead of toward it? And if this is true for me, might it not be a similar truth for all humanity? Here and now I feel as though shackles are removed, but will those shackles be with me again when I return to my own physical time? Is this because we of the current humanity are all juveniles as a species? Or, as I suspect, is it because we have been held back by an unfriendly species that for a very long time has energetically held us as captives within the illusion of freedom?"

For a long moment there is an impenetrable, interminable silence. It could be it lasts a micro-moment, or it could be it lasts a century. In some inexplicable way I am so far removed from the passage of time that I have no way of knowing.

Slowly, as though emerging from a deep sleep—lifetimes of sleep—I am aware of time and space dancing all around me. Literally millions of linear years seem to be dancing with tomorrow, which holds hands with yesterday, in turn becoming this moment.

Five

The humanity you are with now is but the tip of a vast iceberg. Humans are spread throughout the galaxy . . . and beyond.

I BECOME AWARE of myself sitting on a smooth ochre-coloured rock. As I gaze around I am surprised to see what I can only describe as a type of lunar landscape. The vast forest has gone, along with its unique living, thriving, and buoyant energy. Naturally, this landscape also has its own energy, one of loss, faint echoes of what was once a vibrant energy. I see a place where a neutral black energy of Order completely dominates the landscape, and I realise that this desolation is very, very old.

Am I on an asteroid? Or Mars, perhaps . . . or even our moon?

What happened? How, why, did everything change so suddenly? Where is the immense forest of giant trees?

You asked a very different question.

Despite my bewilderment, I am aware of Pan nearby. I cannot see him, of course, but I inner-hear/feel him.

In all our journeys together you have met many metaphysical Beings, and you have never questioned their intent. You have met lower energy Beings with ill intent, reflecting their lower energy, yet always you have emerged from these encounters unscathed and undeterred. I have wondered why you never questioned or, indeed, never looked into the depths of human and so-called alien connections.

"I'm not sure what you are getting at, Pan. I have seen the Greys on the odd occasion and avoided them, or blasted them with Love . . . so to speak, but I think I am missing the point you are trying to get me to see."

Currently in your life, you are realising that other Beings of ill intent are, and for long have been, holding humanity to ransom. Aided and abetted by certain low-energy people, they feed off negative human energy. How did it take you so long to realise that humanity, which is fundamentally a positive species, has developed so slowly in its overall consciousness?

I sigh. Isn't that a good question!

"There is no easy answer. I grew up thinking and accepting that people generally work for the betterment of society as a whole."

And yet your Second World War took place during your childhood, your formative years!

"Look, Pan, I am not attempting to excuse myself, just to explain it. To me, the war just meant that there were goodies and baddies, and that I, and therefore the British were some of the goodies. Simple and trite maybe, but I was just a kid, so the message of the war had little to no impact on me. It just meant that sweets and chocolate were rationed! At home and at school I was subtly taught that the words of authority were always right, and that these should be, and were, my guidelines in life.

"It was only when I emigrated away from the family in England to Oz that I began to change. In Tasmania I began to question the modern farming techniques, eventually emerging as one in the early line-up of organic farmers. This, in turn, led me toward communicating with Nature as I began to 'feel' the connections in all life. As you know, I wrote a book about this, *Talking with Nature,* followed by other such books as I began to explore a greater reality, and yet through all this I never questioned the slow pace of human evolution. I did not give it a thought, or even think that anything was unusual. I consider that I was slow in my spiritual growth, so why should other people not be slow, or even slower? Back then I thought that religion and spirituality went hand in hand . . . until I learned that the opposite is true.

"Today, I look back in wonder! I suspect that I did not want to know about the growing global control by the one percent over the other ninety-nine percent. I did not want to know about the massive corruption and deceit being perpetrated on the people. My oldest son, Duncan, became aware of this long before I did. I thought that he was influenced negatively by other misguided people. Time has proved that I was wrong. The time came, comparatively recently, when I felt compelled to metaphysically investigate the underbelly of humanity. That was when, finally, the plan to control and enslave the human soul itself, became increasingly obvious to me.

"I also realise that if I had discovered all that I now know about the dark side of humanity, before I experienced unconditional Love, I would have been very deeply affected . . . and not for the better. As it is, I have a Love and compassion for humanity, even the malevolent one percent that seek complete domination. When I asked the forest deva my question, all this was behind it. I guess I was looking for confirmation."

What are you asking for? The history of humanity in the cosmos?

I smile to myself.

Although Pan is never with me in any form, metaphysical or otherwise, I am accompanied by his energy. Pan's energy is everywhere at one and the same moment. There is no separate piece of energy for me, yet in the way that the whole ocean is in every drop, so all of Pan is within all of Nature. And we of humanity are not separate from Nature.

"Though you are godlike in comparison to me, even I can feel the humorous sarcasm in the energy of your reply. No, I would not like you to take me through the history of the cosmos. I would die of either old age or boredom long before you finished. Truly, my focus is not on what is wrong with humanity . . . but I would like to know how long we have been held back . . . repressed and controlled . . . and even why?"

I feel an inner chuckle from Pan. *You are prone to sighs of exasperation from time to time. Such a sigh would be timely for me about now, but I am eternal patience. Let me give you a very brief overview of humanity, and of your place in the scheme of things.*

In a way that is impossible to explain, Pan's telepathic words are accompanied by a constantly changing inner vision that greatly expands and emphasises his explanation. I suspect that one day in the so-called future we will communicate in this far more evolved and enlightened manner.

The humanity you are incarnating with now is but the tip of a vast iceberg. Humans are spread throughout the galaxy . . . and beyond. Most have evolved far beyond the status of your current humanity. This does not make you lesser in any way. As you so often say, Earth is a kindergarten. There are very many timelines. Those on earlier timelines have naturally evolved, just as this is your current human destiny, and as it is for those who follow you.

Within this vast scenario, there are also many types of humanoids. By this I mean that the shape follows the general pattern of two legs and two arms connected to a central body and walking upright, but they are not all human by definition. Some of them are insect-like, some are reptilian, some are gigantic while some are tiny. The range is huge. While most are definitely benevolent, some are not. Just as there are human predators, so there are insect-like predators and reptilian predators, plus many, many more species; all humanoid. Add to this the vast numbers of non-humanoid intelligent life-forms, all occupying thousands of timelines simultaneously . . . plus multiple dimensions and parallel worlds, and you have a tiny idea of the vastness and complexity of galactic and universal life.

You will be aware that to this mix you can add a huge amount of deliberately bred hybrids. A mix of many life forms and races. Some have been bred to be warriors, some to be slaves, some to be wise arbitrators, and some an almost random mix of competence and submission. I say all this to offer an insight into the impossibility of attempting to understand, or in any way categorise it.

And finally, this is all happening in just one universe. There are billions of universes. Add to this the many parallel universes and you have the complexity of an infinite number of multiverses!

Now . . . what was it you wanted to know?

I gulp. "All that you just shared is beyond comment. It is just too humbling. Okay, last question. It would seem that we have been under the influence of human/reptilian hybrid predators for a very long time. How do we rise beyond this in our current predicament?"

Mixael, you already know the answer. With others, you willingly came from a fifth dimensional reality to be part of the energy that is able to 'Lovingly' resist and oppose the reptilian influence. Certain well known human bloodlines contain thousands of years of reptilian energy . . . and they seek nothing less than complete domination of humanity. This is the spiritual battle you are now involved in. It is a battle for the human soul. As for how long you remain in thrall to these creatures, and how you rise above and beyond them, this also you know.

"Please, Pan . . . spell it out. Assume that I do not know. And most certainly I do not have your breadth of insight."

Very well. Many of the benevolent species both humanoid and, let us say, alien, long ago came together and formed what you now refer to as the Galactic Federation. With their combined abilities they are a power to be reckoned with. They, in conjunction with predicted astrological and planetary influences, are raising the frequency of the planet Earth and of all its life forms. This has been taking place for well over one hundred of your timeline years. The effect is now becoming obvious. Nature has risen naturally with the frequency, but humans each have to make the choice. Choice is your birthright. Unfortunately, humanity has endured many thousands of years of conditioning, so mass-consciousness subconsciously resists this higher frequency. Equally, millions prevail against their conditioning, gaining some self-mastery, while yet others do not even comprehend or yet realise that anything is happening at all. By default, they take a do-nothing approach. It is an unfortunate trend of humanity to resist and deny that which they do not understand. Humans tend to follow fear, caution and logic rather than

Love, trust, and their intuition.

I sigh. Logic was born from the intellect, while intelligence gives birth to intuition. I consider intuition to be a higher expression of intelligence.

"So is this causing what I call the Great Divide, or am I being overly dramatic?"

I feel the inner-smile again. *It would be fair to say you are being less than dramatic. Humanity is One . . . always. Nevertheless, you are at the point on your timeline where humanity splits into two streams of consciousness, each moving onto its own reality/timeline. There is no saved, no lost. Each to his or her own frequency. The larger stream will not be from conscious choice; it will be largely from subconscious fear, reaction and resistance. The lifetimes of conditioning hold onto more-of-the-same, not realising that major Change is the price all Beings pay for the evolution of the consciousness of soul and spirit.*

"Can I do more to assist in this evolution than I am?"

Your role is to inspire. This is one of your talents. Your energy holds sincerity and Truth, compassion and Love. Those who feel this will be most touched at a soul level, they will be inspired. Those who do not will be more sceptical, requiring proof of your words. Some will be attracted to your energy, while others will be repelled. It is as it is. You are all eternal Beings, and for every single human their time will come.

"But this is a very important time, yes?"

On your timeline it is of immense importance. An event that has been many, many centuries in the making. However, in the grand universal scheme of life it is a mere blink in eternity.

"Thank you, Pan. You have given me a broader picture and awaked me to the deeper awareness of my older memories. Thank you. I'm very well satisfied. We humans tend to get wrapped up in our lives as though we are the focal point in the universe. I mean . . . humanity has long considered the question; are we alone!? It's ridiculous! It seems rather like gazing into a vast ocean without realising that the ocean is composed of an infinite number of drops which together, become the One ocean. It is the same way throughout the galaxy and the vastness of the multiverse; the infinite many in the One. Add to this the fact that we, each one of us, *are* the drops in the ocean, all unknowing. How can humanity know the ocean when we know so little of ourselves?"

How indeed?

I feel the energy of Pan withdraw as I move into a contemplative mood. Not withdraw as in being absent, but rather withdraw from communication. I allow insight to flower as I bring my focus to the words and wisdom of Pan.

A familiar mantra runs through the mind: nothing by accident, nothing by chance. And, like it or not, this includes the whole human condition.

As a spiritual teacher I am very aware of the depths of our victim consciousness in humanity. In the many wonderful Nature videos we see on television, most people immediately identify with the victim in the act of being killed, feeling sorrow and pity for the dying creature. Very seldom do people truly identify with the predator. The grace and power of the predators are very much admired, yes, along with their beauty—although this is not extended to the much disliked hyenas! But the act of killing brings our compassion toward the victim. It is imprinted in us. And this is absolutely okay! In most ways it benefits us.

However, over the vast linear time of our evolution, this has very slowly evolved into our human victim consciousness. Instead of revelling in the inner strength and growth that comes from a challenge, many, even most people have resented being under duress. Not all people, not by any means ... but many people. As life became ever easier for most of us, we became more resistant to *unwanted* tests and challenges that came from various disasters, whether personal or national.

Without going into lengthy explanations, as I am sure you understand me, we have developed a powerful and dominant victim consciousness. The clearest evidence of victim consciousness is the amount of people suing another person, or people; litigation. The world's courts are overflowing with litigations. We always look outside of ourselves to blame someone else, or a corporation. We totally ignore a universal principle that applies to all sentient Beings: *In every moment of your life* you *are creating the content and direction of every moment of your life.* Instead, we blame another. This is the human victim consciousness laid bare.

This victim consciousness has grown and endured for the whole Great Cycle that is now ending . . . approximately 200,000 years. And totally unrealised, it has consumed the huge majority of humanity. It has become part of our subconscious programme . . . to blame. What humanity never seemed to learn is that the victim always attracts a victimiser. This is how life works. If you have a victim consciousness you will get picked on! And even more crazy, you will victimise yourself! It has always been this way. And yet, so few seem to realise this.

The question that arises is simple and basic: how does a species shed from itself an ailment, infirmity, disorder, disability that it does not even know it has? There is an answer. As a soul-species, where each person is creating their own eternal life, the answer is for humanity to co-create together a situation where it becomes obvious that we are 'all' being victimised to some degree or another.

Enter the cabal; the reptilian/human hybrids. They are our victimisers. The 1 percent who have been around for thousands of years. Of course, they did not advertise their role in this. They did exactly the opposite, covertly building huge organisations hoarding the vast wealth they leached from an unaware and victimised public, while developing multinational corporations to gradually take complete control of the world's money and trade. From media to pharmaceuticals, to fuel and agriculture, to distribution and banking, all of it; they now own the two or three huge companies that control the major companies of the world. Along the way, murder and coercion became a common aspect of their vast and complex deceit.

We are now living in a unique time.

The old cycle of cabal dominance is ending, dying . . . finished.

A new cycle is beginning; the Age of Aquarius. A new Golden

Age of Freedom and Prosperity is now violently clashing with a dying dictatorship. As the life-frequency on Earth keeps on rising with the birth of the Golden Age, so for a while the conflict will intensify. The rising Chaos is actually Love driven, breaking down the structures and templates of the old, while the old dominance is doing everything it can to create ever more fear. So there we have it: fear holding the old energies fighting to deny the rising power of Love, the energy of newness.

This unfolding conflict offers everyone the opportunity to see how our subconscious victim-consciousness has been brought into such a powerful manifestation. In many ways, as a collective human consciousness, we created the cabal . . . not that this in any way excuses their ruthlessness, their complete lack of humanity.

Of course, most people will continue to blame, remaining as victims. The timeline is splitting. I foresee that those in denial will leave this timeline, continuing on into more-of-the-same. This is due to their inability to grasp that we each individually, and all collectively, create our own human lives on Earth. This is our lesson to learn. We each create our own life. There is no right and no wrong, there never has been. It is all about lessons: our being conscious, our choices, and the timing.

For those who leave the overwhelming victim-consciousness, taking sovereignty over their own lives, they will undoubtedly inherit this Earth, clean and unpolluted. While the unstoppable Golden Age is still in its very infancy, it follows the natural order of life.

As each person embraces and lives their Truth, so the New unfolds.

Your Truth: You are a magnificent, metaphysical, multidimensional, immortal and eternal Being of Love, the power of creation, and Light, the illumination of eternity.

Six

As you know, the right flow of consciousness comes from needs rather than wants. Needs as for the spiritual Being you are, as opposed to wants as for the physical persona to possess.

WE ARE HAVING a time of rain, which in my garden is always a welcomed event. I would not say that we cannot have too much rain, but on my little mountain we can sure handle a lot with no problems. It all just soaks in! I can hear the garden taking a deep in-breath as it very quietly drinks its fill. This is not so much a sound, as a movement in the energy of the garden. You need to be a conscious gardener to experience this, and sadly these people are becoming less common each year. As technology comes to the aid of the gardener making our lot easier, but subtly more detached, so the unique connection of using quiet muscle power and gentle persuasion in the garden is being lost. And with it goes our conscious connection. Today, most gardeners unwittingly work subconsciously in the garden, using their skills and knowledge in an automatic process that certainly may ensure a very well presented garden, but at the cost of the deeper mystical connection between the person and the spirit of the land.

I was once asked if I could define when I became a gardener. For me, that was an easy question. I was six. My father brought home twelve tomato plants, six for me and six for him. Together we planted them in two separate rows, his and mine. After about two weeks his plants were bigger and greener than mine. By the fourth week it was so obvious that I cried. When I showed him the reason for my tears, he was very perplexed.

"I can't understand it," he said. "Yours don't seem to have grown at all. I wonder why?"

"I don't know why either," I replied. "I dig them up every day to check the roots for growth, but they don't grow."

Dad just smiled . . . and explained about simply *allowing* the plants to grow and *trusting* the process.

I was delighted when, just as his tomatoes had finished fruiting, my tomatoes started bearing a large and tasty crop. The tomato plants were the catalysts that launched me into eventually being a Conscious Gardener. Hence the title of my last and final book on organic gardening.

Now, in my mid-eighties, the twin miracles of *allowing* and *trusting* are the tools I most use both in the garden and in life. I allow my inner-knowing to emerge in all situations and I fully trust it. Most people are so caught up in the pursuit of externalised knowledge that they have completely lost sight of the way life truly works: One humanity, One world . . . no separation. If all is One, all learned knowledge and cognitive knowing is within, not outside of us. Outside of self is the game of the intellect and the ego, doing their best in an attempt to be all important in the overall act of life. In truth, the intellect is more an onlooker of life, a critic, an analyst; never a participant.

This has been the purpose of my life: not so much to understand how it works, but to experience its inner working. What we understand is really the superficial stuff floating on the surface of life. Life is like an ocean. You do not look at the surface of the ocean and think you have seen all of it, for you realise that the depths are vast beyond your sight. Life is like this. We look at human lives, our own lives, and make judgements of life; it is this way, or that, according to our beliefs, cultures, religions, education, attachments and wants, yet this is simply flotsam floating on the surface. Comparatively few people have learned that life is of a vast multidimensional depth and immensity within its many frames of reality.

For most people life is to be physically, mentally and emotionally explored . . . and intellectually understood. And this is okay. It is the comparative few who realise that the exploration of life must be conducted on a deeper metaphysical level, for we are eternal metaphysical Beings, not physical and transient. And yet . . . and yet . . . just as flower buds unfold in perfect timing, so also do we. The difference, however, is that while the sun and rain go far to determine the timing of the flowering of a bud, it is our own focus and intent that determine the timing for the spiritual maturing and flowering of a human Being.

So much is visually obvious, while so very much more is unseen, not at all obvious. Yet, it is the obvious to which most people are drawn, and it is in the obvious where illusion waits to ensnare us. Illusion weaves its webs of deceit and beliefs, and we quickly ensnare ourselves with our emotional attachments.

I sigh. I wish to explore the unseen world that surrounds us. The world that lies beyond the more dense frequency of our vision and sound. Physically, this is held away from us . . . and undoubtedly, this is wise. When you consider our track record of environmental destruction and pollution, the world needs a layer of protection from us. Our basic tenet is; if I cannot see it, it does not exist. Good! Long may this belief continue, even if it is false.

It is a common belief that to experience Nature we need to be out in Nature. This works well enough, but it does contain limitations. And just because we may not be aware of the limitations does not mean that they do not exist! Being in Nature physically tends to hold us within our physical limits. Yes, some people do sit quietly and meditate, and yes, this does take them beyond the physical limits, but again, these people are comparatively few. For every one of these people there are a thousand chattering in their heads while they admire the externalised Nature that surrounds them.

I have discovered that for me, sitting in my study in my comfortable chair, I am able to relax my physical body. When it is fully relaxed—I am not the body!—I am able to leave it as a metaphysical Being and journey into a Nature that is also beyond the physical. Not for a moment am I denying the joy of our physical interaction with a physical Nature, I do this very often . . . in fact, most of the time in my garden. But the metaphysical connection which is lost to most people is, for me, a very revealing, very precious and truly sacred connection. It is at this metaphysical level where the curtains of illusion are pulled right back.

We are all Beings of energy. When I leave the dense energy of my physical body—and we can all do this with practice—I am in the higher frequency of my metaphysical body. (My recent book *Entering the Secret World of Nature* will help you with this.) In daily life the physical and the metaphysical occupy the same moment, yet with practice we can leave our physical body relaxed and move away in our metaphysical body as a whole new world is revealed. This is rather like astral travel, or out-of body experiences, while the body is awake, not asleep. This is a world of a far greater reality; a world where layer upon layer of ever higher frequencies of unrealised reality all occupy the same space/moment. Seriously . . . we are not metaphysical prisoners in a physical body, even though this is normal, everyday life for most people.

* * *

One brisk day in our subtropical winter, the southerly wind keeping the temperature decidedly cool, I metaphysically leave my physical body relaxed in the study as I saunter/drift through my large, tree-studded garden.

Of course, the temperature makes no difference to my metaphysical self. It could be freezing or scorching, this is all physical. Equally, I have no need to breathe, this accompanies the physical body. Nevertheless, I am aware of the movement of breathing in my physical body and, oddly, I find it strangely comforting. I can see all around me, also above and below, all in one simultaneous moment.

Metaphysically, this is natural rather than deliberate, just as seeing through my physical eyes in everyday life is natural, rather than deliberate. However, although I do not need a two-eye focus, I find that I am looking around me in the way of being physical. Interestingly, I can see through this focus, but in a different and far more holistic way. A sense of greatly expanded freedom sweeps through me.

I have a suspicion that what I am hoping to do is going to be rather challenging. My normal metaphysical journeys are mostly in other realms of reality; such as the various levels of the astral. I have briefly explored the higher and lower mental and emotional planes of human astral existence, encountering some very strange experiences.[1] Add to this my exploring a mere fraction of the astral realms of Nature, with their incredible Spirits of Nature. Equally, I have had several galactic experiences, exploring tiny sections of our solar system. But always I was so far from my normal and familiar that I was prepared for anything.

Now however, I am hoping to find and explore the familiar areas of my garden . . . but on a higher frequency, or frequencies. I am hoping to leave behind all that is familiar in my everyday relationship with the physical frequency of my 2.4 acres of garden, and explore the garden space that has a frequency faster than the speed of light. What will I encounter? I literally have no clue, no idea. My experience so far is that the pull of the physically familiar is challenging to break through. How do I see beyond the known into the unknown when I am surrounded by the known? I have never before made a decision to move beyond my regular metaphysical focus . . . and now, this is what is required. It is a bit like knowing that we are able to physically see at a higher level than normal, but have no clue how to do it!

This is my current dilemma. How do I do this?

It is definitely time to call for Pan!

Not for a moment do I believe that this utterly amazing universal

---

1. Both the astral encounters and the galactic experiences are to be found in my book, *Stepping . . . Between . . . Realities*.

Intelligence is unaware of my predicament.

But as I project my own signature . . . *help* . . . I am hoping that he will respond. He likes me to push my limits!

Suddenly . . .

You really should know how to do this.

"What . . . you have never taught me!"

Did I teach you to walk through linear time without the need to wade through it as though pushing through oceanic waves of resistance?

"Ah, well . . . that was different."

Oh . . . how so?

I sigh. "You know perfectly well that I was in a hurry, so I momentarily forgot that I could not simply step between realities."

And so you did.

"Um, well, yes, I did."

Perhaps you could also forget your way into higher frequencies.

"Very funny! Oh, come on. Give me a break."

I inner-feel energetic waves of mirth.

You need to discover the secret to the secret in your heart.

"Er . . . if it's a secret how do I do that?"

That, my friend, is yet another secret . . . and yours to discover.

※　　※　　※

Interestingly and rather surprisingly, this is where our conversation ended. It was like an odd stalemate which Pan refused to break. I had an intuitive knowing that I had to give it time. To metaphysically stand within the familiar known while seeking the greater unknown defeated me. I did not know how to begin. Prior to this, being metaphysical was the key, always, but now I was seeking the metaphysical beyond my *known* metaphysical. A sort of back to the unknown once again, but on a higher level.

However, it was another six months before—with no clue of my dilemma—my dear friend Elisabeth Karsten while online from Germany asked me if I knew anything about the 5th chamber of the heart.

I did not! As she asked me, I had goosebumps creeping over my neck, so all my attention was riveted on her next words as she briefly described it. She then sent me the internet link where I was able to read about the physical aspects of the 5th chamber. Medically it is known as the vagus node, or nerve. It is very small, about 4mm. When a special hi-tech camera and lens for photographing into the cells of the body were used, the image of a very tiny, atom-sized androgynous human was revealed. This prompted it to be called the God atom! Even more surprising is the fact that while the bodies' normal temperature is around 35 degrees Celsius, within the 5th chamber it is, apparently, 100 degrees Celsius!

Naturally enough, I was very soon investigating this on a metaphysical level . . . and here I found the secret buried within the human heart.

To find the 5th chamber I metaphysically walk through the four chambers of my large metaphysical Heart House, making sure that the rooms are all in perfect order and vibrant with energy. I have no idea how I am going to find the 5th chamber which I have never yet seen, so I do not know where to look. Consequently, I decide to let it find me. My intent is clear and focussed, so all I need to do is keep any stray thoughts out of the way. *Trust* and *allow* come strongly into play!

The first room is my Childhood Trauma which I have previously transformed into my room of Childhood Triumph. This is just as I had left it; active, thriving, and definitely honouring the five-year-old me. The second room was my Self-Sabotage when I first entered. With effort, I transformed it into the room of Self-Sovereignty. It is magnificent. Very honouring.

The third room when I first encountered it was Wants and Poverty. This I transformed into the room of Appreciation and Abundance. My steady Waterfall of Supply is flowing into the Pool of Plenty and flowing on out into the world. Finally, I walk into the fourth room of Spiritual Wisdom. This had never been tarnished, always light-filled and sparkling with energy. Here, using my metaphysical forefinger like a stylus, I have written some of the Principles of Truth in my very heart centre . . . where they belong.

Okay, now what? Glancing around my room of Spiritual Wisdom, I am startled to see a door that has never before been here. It is a handsome door, made from some type of wood and covered in carvings. Staring at them, I have the feeling that they are meaningful rather than random, but I have no idea of their meaning. I cautiously open the door and walk through it. Before me there is a long corridor, filled with radiant Light. I am in no hurry, so I walk slowly feeling the powerful energy all around me. Ahead of me I can see a very large door that is clearly unable to fully contain the Light behind it. It is as though the Light is blasting through weak areas of the door, and I know that when, or if, I open that door, the Light will be overwhelmingly powerful. And . . . hot?

On reaching the door, I stop with some apprehension. I have no idea what this door is made of. If I had to guess it would be of thickly and densely woven cobwebs, but that is ridiculous . . . surely!

Even though I can be cautious, it never lasts long, so fully in character I fling the door open . . . and it is as light as a feather! The Light, which feels like living energy, blasts out, and I can feel tremendous heat . . . and yet, it does not burn, and the Light . . . it does not blind. I am okay!

I literally feel an invitation to walk into . . . whatever. So I walk into the centre of a star, a sun, I know not, only that it is hot, incomprehensibly vast, and Light. Light which is brilliant illumination, rather than Light from any one or more sources. The heat and Light is so intense it even penetrates my tingling metaphysical body, but all without any stress or trauma for me. In fact, I feel . . . wonderful . . . powerful. I feel enabled.

Now, finally, I am ready and able to enter that which has always been metaphysically beyond me, beyond my reach, beyond my abilities.

Finally, with clarity and purpose, I am able to inner-leap powerfully from the 5th chamber of my heart . . . into a magnificent city!

* * *

A city, how is this possible? A city of such illumination and power that for a few faltering moments has me thinking that I am maybe lost in the vast metaphysical chamber of my heart.

But no. I am standing in the physical area of my large garden, even though there is no sign of it. In this higher frequency my garden is as unseen as the city is from my physical garden. Astonishing . . . and all occupying the same space/moment on entirely different frequencies. Although I mentally *knew* different realities occupy the same space/moment, to witness and experience it is another level of *knowing* entirely. It is akin to seeing the first touches of dawn light outside your bedroom window as the morning sun rises, and then drawing back the curtains to reveal what has been hidden by the darkness of the night.

Although it quickly becomes apparent that the small city is very much bigger than my garden, I inner-know that my garden is in the very heart of the city. Wow! I truly had no expectations because this was such an unknown reality for me that I did not even speculate. But a city of what seems to be glass . . . this leaves me utterly amazed. And the energy! I feel myself to be trembling in my metaphysical body at the sheer beauty and deep, vibrant energy of this incredible place.

"Okay Pan, it took a while, but I found the secret in the heart and here I am. Any chance of you joining me and . . . well, accompanying me?"

Do I ever truly leave? I am within the very pulse of life. I was with you as you first entered the chamber and I am with you now.

"Er . . . I knew that, but I like to hear you communicating with me. It is very reassuring. I confess, I was so overwhelmed within the chamber that I was unaware of you. How amazing that such a tiny physical vessel could be so utterly vast on a metaphysical level. I imagine you are aware that the microscopic androgynous human image they found in the chamber is being referred to as the God atom."

A typical human conclusion to verify a fabricated belief. God is in the shape of Divine Love, of Supreme Intelligence, of Universal Truth. Humanity and Nature are indeed all this, even if it is still in a limited, embryonic state of expression.

"Oh!" I am so surprised by his words I have no comment to make. But I recover fast!

"Er . . . how would you refer to it?"

If you remember, I suggested that you find the secret to the secret in your heart. You have found the secret, but have you found the secret to the secret?

With his telepathic words I feel an incredible penetrating energy. It feels as though a Serpent of Light is uncoiling and slithering from my solar plexus chakra up to my heart chakra. I become aware of a realisation that has hovered around me ever since the moment I first entered the 5th chamber.

"Oh my God . . . yes, I have. For years I have been teaching people that you are the world, that you are the universe . . . and I felt it, but now, suddenly, this inner-knowing has jumped to a far higher, more holistic level. I am in the universe and the universe is within me . . . within the 5th chamber."

To say that I am feeling ecstatic is putting it mildly. I inner-feel a connection that has always, somehow, evaded me on this much deeper level. We all think far too much. We overthink everything! We think ourselves away from Truth, away from universal discoveries, away from all our many natural connections in life, away from our eternal, holistic, greater spiritual world.

I inner-feel Pan chuckling. *If I tell you that your 5th chamber is the Seed of Ascension, it will now make sense.*

I have tears trickling down my physical cheeks. "Oh Pan, has anything in all my many incarnations ever made better sense? Never! Talk about Truth in perfect timing. You grow me in much the same way as I grow my plants. I am watered when I need it for my growth, and fertilised with exactly what I need for my flowering. Thank you, my beloved teacher. Thank you so much."

For long moments Pan says nothing as I stand feeling my emotions of such intense gratitude that this incredible energy we call Pan actually Loves me, nurtures me, cares for me . . . that I am choked up. I am not demeaning myself, just emotionally overwhelmed that a magnificent universal energy of such immensity can recognise and nurture the magnificence within me.

I sigh. I am more used to being the gardener than the garden!

"I imagine that I can step from the 5th chamber to anywhere and any-when in the universe, so long I am in the right flow of consciousness."

This is correct. As you know, the right flow of consciousness comes from needs rather than wants. Needs as for the spiritual Being you are, as opposed to wants as for the physical persona to posses."

"Yes, no right or wrong, just different states of consciousness."

I drag my focus away from inner revelations back to this remarkable city I have entered. I feel no haste or hurry. For years I have wondered just why the energy on our little mountain ridge is so powerful. In the same way, what is it that makes one place of no great physical attributes so much more powerful than another, often more beautiful place? I have long suspected that power can seep from a magnificent higher energy expression on a higher vibrational frequency to other less distinguished areas. And yet, the power here is subtly different from the energy of the mountain ridge in my reality. Higher, certainly, but not better . . . just different.

Indeed, this is what I'm discovering on our little mountain ridge. Whereas I am no lover of cities—I avoid them if at all possible—this city I am standing within is as far from being an ordinary city as a sparrow is from being an albatross.

Interestingly, with all the universe on offer, as it were, your choice is to see the many levels of the comparatively microscopic piece of land on which you live.

"Hmm . . . as a universal energy you may see it that way, but for me this quite large piece of land comprised of our house and garden is our much loved home. I have let go of my earlier emotional attachments to it, so now I am free to simply enjoy living here and caring for our home." [2]

---

[2]. For a couple of years now I have been presenting a Healing Humanity online meditation on the first Sunday of every month on Zoom. This is one of my online contributions toward the very much needed raising of the human consciousness in these times of Change and spiritual Awakening. If you are aware of this, then you will know that I often take the meditators into the 5th chamber and link it with the pineal, which is the Third Eye, and the sun in the 12th chakra. I strongly recommend this as it is very powerful and effective. This meditation is also available from the Michael Roads Online Community on the Mighty Network. Also available is the 'Heart House' meditation for metaphysical and physical heart healing, as mentioned in this chapter.

Seven

Please do not feel offended, but your approach to our level of reality has all the sounds of an aircraft leaving one of your airports. You live in a very noisy frame of reality. What you consider to be silence to us is the horrendous thunder of billions of people's thinking gone mad.

Even though I am aware of being in the centre of the city, I see no people. Peering up at the buildings, I try to imagine what they really are, or what they are here for, or what they contain. Our normal cities have a large amount of buildings filled with offices and businesses, rising for many storeys above the streets, while the lower floors are for a large variety of shops, along with food and coffee places to entice people off the streets to sample their merchandise. This is nothing like that. Is it even a city? When I stepped from the 5th chamber to stand among these buildings, I instantly assumed it to be a city, but now I am having second thoughts. Who ever heard of glass buildings? I know that our architects use a lot of glass in our ultra-modern buildings, but these are *all* glass, even the construction . . . or so it seems! I realise that I need to slow down within my speculation. I am looking through the consciousness of old eyes, of old knowledge, of attempting to mentally understand.

I have encountered many very strange buildings in my various metaphysical travels, particularly an astral one that had its own Beingness, its own intelligence. That one was a real shock. Apparently, I was fortunate that it decided to release me. So what is my problem here? I suspect that I am thinking in very human terms . . . after all, I do this in my daily reality! But here, I need to think in terms of 'what is' rather than how I expect it to be.

Walking toward a building, I first encounter what seems to be a path, so I step onto it rather gingerly. As I do so, I feel a tingle of energy ripple through my metaphysical body. Okay . . . I did not expect that! I have the distinct feeling that I am being assessed. This puzzles me, so I stand still, not sure how to proceed. With no prompting from me, the path moves me very gently toward the building. How does it know that I want to touch the building? I realise that while this 'city' is probably attuned to human needs, but surely not the human needs of my timeline reality. It suddenly occurs to me that this is another city with intelligence. With this in mind, I ask the path if I am correct. Instantly, I have a very clear affirmation. There are no words, no razzmatazz, just a clear inner certainty that seems to have been implanted in me without thought. This is very intriguing.

"Please . . . er, path," I ask, "would you be kind enough to introduce me to this city? I belong to a different, more dense frequency. I am here in my metaphysical body . . . and I need help."

With my request, a flow of inner-knowing seems to be ignited. I realise that if I focus on my intent, I will be continually in the flow of this city. It seems that it *is* a city! I am glad to have that sorted out! So, maintaining a focus on wishing to touch the structure of the building that is closest to me, I am delighted to find that the path is steadily carrying me toward my destination. When I first arrived here, and based on my everyday reality, I decided that the city is glass. Now, as I steadily draw closer, I suspect that I might need a completely new appraisal. It is looking a lot less like glass in every moment. The path is an enigma in itself! I am being carried toward the building, but the path is not moving, not a single part of it. This is nothing like the big people-movers in our airports. I do not have a clue how this is happening. As Alice would say, "Curiouser and curiouser!"

I arrive close to a building and, taking a few more steps off the path, I reach out and touch it. I have no idea what to expect, but touch can reveal quite a lot about the energy of whatever it is you touch. Instantly, it becomes obvious that this building is alive. It is as obvious as touching a sleeping cat or cow, except this building is not sleeping.

Welcome. We have been expecting you.

"Oh . . . er . . . thank you. Expecting me! How is that possible?"

While the people of your consciousness are not aware of us, we have an awareness of those of you who are more spiritually enlightened. In this way we have been cognisant of your interest in extending your metaphysical boundaries. In many ways, this is a remarkable moment.

"You say we . . . but there is no one here."

If a building can chuckle, this building just did.

Please do not feel offended, but your approach to our level of reality has all the sounds of an aircraft leaving one of your airports. You live in a very noisy frame of reality. What you consider to be silence to us is the horrendous thunder of billions of people's thinking gone mad.

"Oh my gosh, you can hear us thinking?"

Only when we choose to, and this is rare. But we have been listening to the rumble of your thoughts as you approached this moment.

"Hmm . . . this is rather embarrassing."

Please do not be embarrassed by my comments. We are more forthright than you are used to simply because all our communications are telepathic, thus emotions and thoughts merge into a far more efficient and less personal way of communication. Offensive and defensive are nothing more than concepts for us, because we share and experience a higher consciousness of Love.

"So, if I say that you are just a building, that will not be offensive?"

Are you implying offence?

"No, not at all. Look, I'm sorry, I'm trying to understand how a . . . a building is so full of knowledge and insight. When you refer to 'us', do you mean the whole city is sentient . . . as you obviously are? For me to refer to 'us' means I am referring to people, humanity. But I have seen no people here. This is why I am confused."

A wave of compassion sweeps through me . . . but this is compassion for me!

Allow us to apologise to you. We have just realised how deeply out of phase you are with this higher reality. We invite you to step through the doorway on your left and we will address this, our oversight. It is no excuse, but a visitor such as yourself is rather rare.

Quite honestly, I have a sense of relief as I step through the doorway and into the building. I like to think that I am reasonably aware, but so far I am feeling increasingly like a moron.

As I enter the building, a clear whitish light settles over me, and I feel a very distinct chill as the light penetrates my metaphysical body. It is as though I am emerging from a dream, where nothing made any sense at all.

"Oh my gosh! I can see."

All around me there are people! Not huge numbers of people, but maybe dozens of them, and they are all looking very concerned. I can only assume that they have been with me ever since I arrived. I smile. Maybe they were equally puzzled by me seemingly ignoring them.

A tall slim man with truly radiant energy walks toward me.

"Is this better? I apologise, but we are not used to contending with metaphysical visitors from lower frequencies."

"Does this mean that you *are* used to receiving metaphysical visitors from higher frequencies?" I ask.

"Of course. This is quite a normal and regular occurrence. You, however, have achieved something that is rather unique. If you do not mind my asking, how did you ever find us?"

"Hmm . . . simple really. I decided to explore the next frequency above my own familiar metaphysical frequency."

The man laughs. "Oh . . . I see. I need to explain to you that you have jumped at least two levels of frequency higher than you expected. No wonder you were out of phase. That is quite an achievement, literally. I doubt that any one of us could metaphysically jump two levels higher than our current frequency."

To say that I am surprised is putting it mildly. I did not know that such a thing was possible.

"When I think back, I realise that I did take a powerful leap from my frame of reality to enter your frame of reality . . . which was this city. Maybe I should have just strolled, but I did not know that an over-jump was possible. I thought it would take effort."

By now there is quite a crowd standing around me, staring as though they have never seen anything like me. It is a bit disconcerting.

"I have a question. Was I communicating with the building, or you? I am feeling rather muddled about this."

"First, allow me to introduce myself. My name is Giles, and I have a position of authority in this city. Let me hasten to add that this is not authority in the way you use the term in your reality. By authority I mean that I am one of the people who maintains the energy-meld between the sentient city and the people who live here. It is basically self-supporting, but I am one of those who deals with any little glitches that may occur."

"Like me" I suggest with a smile.

Giles laughs heartily. I like his energy. It is strong, clear and light, but holds plenty of focus and determination.

"Not really, no. You are not so much a glitch as a phenomenon," he says chuckling. "And, let me assure you, a very welcome one. Just by being here you issue a challenge to some of us to perform a similar feat. I know this is not a challenge from you, but you have inadvertently opened a door of possibilities that we have never truly explored.

"However, come with me from the entrance to a more comfortable room and I will do some introductions with people you may like to meet."

We are, of course, still standing in the doorway of the building, so I follow him and smile to myself as everyone gives me plenty of space. I have no idea how they see me, how formed I may appear or how nebulous. As we walk, I feel/inner-hear a very deep, soft purring sound, like a very contented cat. And I somehow *know* that it is the building!

The people all appear to be rather youngish, in their 30s to 50s. I later learn that some of them are a few hundred years old. Hmm, they sure wear better than we do, but that should not be too surprising. The youthfulness of the older people certainly puts me in my place as an octogenarian. I thought that I was in good shape, but these people are in a whole higher category. I wish I could describe the energy difference between this frequency range and ours, but I have to resort to comparison: this place is total harmony and balance to my senses, compared to our almost total lack of it. Only a few hundred thousand, maybe even a million people in my frequency may have this energy of harmony and balance with life.

We are now in a room that is completely circular, but the room appears to be a garden, even though I inner-know that it is a room. Not only a garden, but a garden that ticks every box in me of the garden that most delights.

"I take it that the sentient building has been reading my energy and knows my preferences of gardens, and that this room duplicates it?"

Giles looks very surprised. "Yes, exactly correct. I had no idea that such things are possible in your frame of reality."

I smile at him. "They are not, but this is not the only place that I have visited. You may be surprised by what is out there in the vast range of greater astral realities and probabilities."

"Ah . . . yes, thank you. You are not exactly a true representation of your people. That is so easy to overlook that I am already jumping to false conclusions based on what we know of your realm."

"The caterpillar knows nothing of the butterfly, but the butterfly is very familiar with the energy of the caterpillar," I tell him. "But then again, there are many species of caterpillars and the subsequent butterflies!"

Giles laughs. "Okay, I suspect that we may learn as much from you as you undoubtedly will from us. I look forward to our mutual sharing."

Many of the people are now sitting in super-comfortable-looking chairs that appear to float. I have encountered such elsewhere, so with no hesitation I sit and relax. To be honest, I do not need to sit, for I seldom feel any fatigue in my metaphysical body, but physiologically it feels good.

A slim and beautiful woman who appears to be in her fifties comes to me. "Hello, and welcome. My name is Melle. We are going to share food and drink. I am guessing that you will be unable to share this with us. Please let me know if this is incorrect."

"Hello Melle, my name is Mixael, and you are right, it is unlikely that I can eat or drink here, and it is entirely unnecessary for me. But, thank you. I would like to ask you a question. How do you see me, or should I say, how do I appear to you? Do I look as physical to you as you do to me?"

She smiles, hesitating. "When you first appeared among us, we were startled. You seemed like us, but very, very hazy. It quickly became apparent that your energy was very different, and that you could neither see nor hear us. We also realised that you were communicating with the sentient building where we are now seated. As you came in here and that Light brought you into phase with us, you appeared to be somewhat more ethereal than us, even though with a strong hint of physicality within you." She sighs! "This is rather difficult to explain. You look like us but without our solidity."

I laugh. "You don't look particularly solid to me. You look like a super version of us; super fit, super healthy and with a super energy. To me you are all slender, healthy and fit, while the overall humanity of my time is anything but healthy and fit . . . with exceptions, of course."

Melle nods knowingly. "I must not monopolise you," she says with a smile, and moves off to mix with other people.

* *You are conducting yourself like a seasoned and veteran traveller of other realms. We find that fascinating. As you have now learned, 'we' is all the non-human sentient life in this reality. However, despite our many different expressions, we are One with humanity. I see that you have an awareness of this in your energy, and you experience Oneness to some degree, but your energy also indicates that this is not common* *among your people.**

I reply to the building telepathically. "Many people have a concept of Oneness and accept its reality, even if they experience it only fleetingly. The majority of people are lost and isolated in the sticky web of separation."

A succession of people come to me and introduce themselves. They are very relaxed, even though curious about me. All of them are beautiful. They radiate a high level of vitality and energy, and even passion that far surpasses people of my reality. I learn about their age in casual conversation. My age seems to surprise them, not that I am young by comparison with them—Melle is 151 years, not about 50 as I expected—but apparently in their knowledge of us, I should be getting doddery in my mid-80s. I have a good laugh over that. I am not yet ready for doddery!

When I describe all of these people as beautiful, I should explain that this is more energetic than physical, even though they are all physically beautiful. But beauty is in the eye of the beholder, so different people see beauty in different ways. For me, the aliveness, the passion, and the relaxed intensity—an oxymoron, sorry!—and the awareness each of them have is both beautiful in their features and in their field of energy. I have learned that true beauty is more than skin deep; real beauty is a state of consciousness.

I am not sure about the passage of time here. I know that I have limits on how long I can be here. Not that this is exhausting, but I am not in the frequency that is natural to me. So, when Giles approaches and offers to give me a quick tour of the city, I instantly accept.

I smile at him. "Do we walk . . . or ride?"

"I have taken the liberty of asking the path to take charge of our tour. The non-human sentient life very quickly established a connection with you while we stood around rather nonplussed by your appearance."

I chuckle. "Very appropriate. I agree, they did make me feel welcome and relaxed . . . even if I was rather puzzled by the lack of people . . . which was my lacking, not yours!"

"Maybe, but we could have been quicker on the uptake. To us, you were a huge surprise. To the city you were another visitor, even if unusual."

Walking onto the path we are moved swiftly and smoothly while we also walk at an easy, steady pace. The effect is rather like a moving walkway at our airports, but smoother, swifter . . . and with intelligence. By this, I mean that the path does not move. Okay, a paradox!

We are approaching a small lake over which our path is a bridge. Your love of goldfish and koi is also noted, so make sure to look into the water.

Sure enough, a small but exquisite lake seems to be gliding smoothly toward us as in reality, we approach it. The path continues over the bridge, and when we are about halfway across the path brings us to a standstill. Giles looks momentarily confused, whereupon he smiles. "I'm impressed. You are in fairly constant communication with the city, while I have only just learned of your love of exotic fish.

"As I said earlier, I have met several intelligent cities, but this one is the most understanding of my humanness; the best ever." So saying I peer into the water. There are no railings here, nothing to stop you falling into the water if you misstep or stumble, but these people do neither. The path holds them . . . without holding them! Okay, another paradox!

Below me, gliding through the water there are koi, magnificent beyond any koi I have ever seen, stunningly vibrant. And there are, or were when I visited, some beauties in the French Island of Guadalupe, and the Hawaiian Island of Maui. But these koi almost glow with health and vitality, and the red and white colours are literally luminous. I should not compare, but I do it only to give you an idea of what I am seeing and experiencing. Like with ours, these koi seem to enjoy shoaling and there must be hundreds, all well over a metre in length. I am reminded just how much I enjoy them. Probably more so because in Queensland, Oz, where I live, we are not allowed to keep koi. Other states have them, but here they fear that they will get into the river system and make it impossible for native fish to thrive. I do not agree with this policy, but I accept it. Victoria has rivers filled with carp, and their native fish have definitely suffered. When koi become wild in the river they inbreed, slowly reverting back to their original carp form and a brownish dull colour.

As we continue, we pass many buildings and places that look like our plazas and shopping centres, but I have the feeling they are somehow very different than ours.

"Surely you don't have shopping centres like us?"

"No, not like yours. These are distribution centres. People can come here for food and home supplies, as well as garden or recreation supplies. No money is used, nothing is bought or sold. Everyone has their own unique way of contributing to our society and everyone thrives in a non-competitive totally supportive way of living."

"What, no credit cards," I chuckle. "So, what is your currency?"

"Mutual support and trust. Love and compassion. Sharing and caring," Giles says quietly, but strongly.

I sigh. "You are Light years beyond us . . . but our turn will come."

"We live in the way of a large family, or tribe. If, on the rare occasions a person does not fit in with the people of a certain place, with blessings and goodwill they go forth and quite easily find their own tribe."

I smile. "Hmm . . . interesting. In my own frame of reality we are going through a major upheaval in consciousness. Although the word 'tribe' has been around almost forever, it is undergoing a more modern definition and meaning as people of a higher consciousness come together, declaring that these people are my tribe. Meaning, of course, mental, emotional, spiritual and ideological compatibility.

"Come to think of it, do you know anything about us? After all, we are neighbours on a lower frequency."

Giles hesitates. "Without intending to sound demeaning in any way, we know a bit about you, but not as much as we know about the higher levels. This, of course, is because we get higher level visitors, and never any visitors from lower levels . . . until now!"

I nod. "Obviously you are on a different timeline from us. Are you in our so-called future, or on a parallel-to-us time? In other words, do you have any insight to the outcome of the metamorphosis we are going through? I could tell you about the control, the lies and deceit of those in power, but I would have to also include the victim consciousness of the mainstream mass of people. Is this perhaps, in your history?"

Giles gestures toward a bench within the botanical park we are walking through. I sigh. Gosh, if only I could take a wheelbarrow full of some of these amazing plants back into my reality. But I doubt they would grow, the energy here is higher with obviously higher energy plants . . . I guess!

As we sit down once more, Giles looks contemplative.

"We exist in your so-called future, yet we also occupy the same space/moment on a higher frequency. Just as you travelled here, so we also travel into higher frequencies than ours. Almost always this is done in vehicles which displace linear time, meaning we arrive in a higher frequency at roughly the same time we leave here. Just as you did in arriving here. However, you travelled energetically, for us this is by no means common. Only a few who are trained are able to do this.

"You ask if I have knowledge of your current situation of major Change. Yes, it is in our history that the timeline splits over the period of years. For those of a higher consciousness, a timeline of a greater potential enfolds them. For those who are stuck in the subconscious murk, the old timeline continues for their future resolution. No death, or lost or saved. No better or worse, or right or wrong. I realise you know this," he adds, holding up his hand to stall my words, "but I want to be clear on these issues. What your human frequency is going through is mainly about the rebirth of your spiritual potential, your innate divinity, which for so long has been suppressed."

"A spiritual renaissance," I tell him. "Long, long overdue!"

He nods again, smiling at me. "Our history would agree with you."

For a moment, he seems to go out of focus, and I realise that this higher frequency is tiring me. Surely it should be the other way around?!

Giles confirms my thoughts. "You are losing stability. Undoubtedly another visit to the Light ray will empower you again, but that might not be wise in the long term."

I nod. "Definitely not a good idea. However, I would like to return here sometime if that is okay with you." I smile wistfully. "I only wish I could bring a camera."

"Do you know how to return to your frequency?" Giles asks. "If so, I will leave you to quietly depart, rather than turn it into a spectator sport."

I laugh. "Amazing, I was about to suggest the same thing. Although I have never done this before, I am hoping to step between frequencies. It works with realities, so why not frequencies? They both seem to share similar characteristics."

Giles stares at me, shaking his head. "You really are a one off."

We hug, sort of, and he continues on through the park. Wow . . . no fuss. This is far better than I expected. But before I go I have a few questions, before I farewell the sentient city.

"In my world reality we are just now grappling with the idea of the safety of artificial intelligence. We have novels and movies that depict AI turning on the humans and enslaving them. Has such a thing ever happened here, or could it?"

It never has and never will. We are sorry to say that such a fear is entirely fitting with the paranoia of your earlier human timeframe. Along with blame, fear was always the reason for war and aggression.

"Hmm . . . a good summary. But how do you know of our history?"

Consider that the non-human sentience in this frequency has a mainframe-base that could be compared to the brain in your body. With a faulty or damaged brain, your body will malfunction. For this reason, your brain is enclosed in a bone skull that offers a reasonable level of protection. Our mainframe-base is enclosed in such a way that offers a very high degree of protection. However, it is regularly updated with regards to historical content, along with recent human discoveries and inventions.

I get the feeling that I am missing something.

Sentience is a controversial subject in your time. Some assume that it offers no more than feelings and sensations, while others consider it as an early stage in the development of consciousness. Not surprisingly, the philosophers of your time view it from their own personal intellectual development, rather than from a place of open intelligence.

I chuckle. "We could talk long on this subject. In my timeline people often do not know the difference between the intellect and intelligence. Some languages actually have no difference for reference. Many people even believe that we each have an intelligence quotient! Most people still do not know that you can only access true intelligence consciously, and not while you are subconscious."

With sentience we are able to contemplate and speculate on any subject. This, in itself, is conscious evolution. Whatever definition they place on sentience in your timeline, we have lifted it to a far higher level. Your visit has ensured that we will have much to contemplate and speculate upon.

"Thank you for all your help. And if truth be known, I was feeling a bit helpless when you first communicated with me. I hope to be with you again in the not too distant future."

We would like that. Just send the thought/intent and we will be ready and waiting for you.

Knowing that the city and path would not, could not, leave, I was a bit self-conscious about my departure. Mostly, returning for me is far easier, as I tire a bit metaphysically and I am going back to my own frequency and my own physical body. All this has a type of vibrational attraction which I feel almost constantly when I metaphysically travel.

*   *   *

So, I did what I now know to be best and stepped . . . between . . . with my home as my focus of destination.

It worked!

Eight

As you leave the consciousness of the collective beliefs and concepts of life, you are far more free to make an assessment of a situation independent of the forgone and emotionally attached conclusions of the collective.

Pan asked the expected question a few days after my return.
So what is the main thrust of all that you learned in that higher frequency realm?

"Hmm . . . it was not so much what I learned that impressed me. It was more that the overall experience confirmed an almost impossible to grasp concept, that on other frequencies this same garden space holds totally different realities. Even though I was fairly certain that it would be so, the reality of it is still overwhelming. It makes me realise just how confined and narrow our overall belief system really is. I realise and accept that we are in our own particular three dimensional reality to learn our own particular lessons, but it feels wrong that we have lived for so long with such incredible limitations. I mean here it is a sclerophyll forest, while there it is part of a living city in the same space! I will write about it, but who will believe it?"

All those who are ready to shed such limitations. Besides which, I am sure you will find stranger realities yet.

"You say that as though you know it to be true."

Mixael, I am a universal and multidimensional energy of Oneness!

"Yes . . . well, there is that! You are something that is so strange in this reality, I am often inclined to overlook the magnitude of your scope."

A month passes by.

My inner work with the Holy Trinity of the Divine Self has progressed very well. Perhaps I should explain this: I discovered that by moving my consciousness through my chakras I was able to take the intense miniature sun from the twelfth chakra, and the third eye from the brow chakra into the vast fifth chamber of my heart chakra. By holding them above my head, together they formed the Holy Trinity of the Divine Self. This is our own deep spiritual essence. By doing this consciously it brings back the Self-empowerment and Truth of Self that we long ago surrendered to religion. We do not need an intermediary between us and the Divine. This creates and empowers separation.

There are now many people in various countries who, having formed small groups, do weekly Healing Humanity meditations. Equally, there are numerous people who do this on a daily basis on their own. The more Love energy that flows into humanity the better. We need it. For me, finding the fifth chamber was another turning point in both inner and outer healing, even though the inner self and the outer Self is One!

Although there are some seriously weird and different hearts out there in the insect world, I have learned that the only other creature that has an actual fifth chamber to its heart is the bee. This intrigues me. Why us . . . and the bee? We are very different! This is surely a question for Pan.

So, I ask my question.

Unlike humans, bees are brilliant communicators. Humans do not consciously listen to each other, nor do they verbalise or articulate with great clarity. Humans speak <u>at</u> each other, rather than <u>to</u> each other, plus they often seem to assume that the other person knows what they are thinking. Overall, humans are poor communicators. I could continue . . . !

"Yes, I'm sure you could. I know that people generally are poor communicators, but that was not my question. My question was why do bees have a fifth chamber to their heart? To me, it is clear that we have the fifth chamber for the purpose of our divinity. I love what you said about it being the Seed to Ascension, but I would hardly apply that to a bee!"

I feel the inner-smile.

Obviously, this has to do with communication. The bee uses the fifth chamber to add a vibrant energy and meaning to the various tones used in its many differing levels of communication. This means that far beyond your audible range, the tones and frequencies of a bee are constantly changing as they communicate. This variable audible range is mixed in with intricate movements of antennae and legs, along with subtle movements of the body and wings. Bees use many levels of highly refined and elusive means of communication to convey directions, wind speed, dangers and pollen type to the other worker bees who are visiting the flowers.

"I use a GPS and still manage to get lost when our car goes through an underground tunnel, or the GPS is not updated and I end up on a dwindling forest track. I guess the bees update each other constantly, while I wait until I get lost a few times. How smart I am!"

The bees update each other after every flight. Remember that the consciousness of the bees is One, and that they are not in the stage of developing individuality as humans are. Humans think and act alike while believing that they are all different and unalike . . . with exceptions! The energy in the tiny fifth chamber of the heart of each bee carries a quality that binds the bees together, yet also allows them each the freedom of their own expressions of being a bee. However, these expressions of independence would be impossible for human science to detect, it is there as an energy. Despite this, as a swarm they are totally dependent on each other to make the hive a holistic whole.

"Hmm . . . you surprise me. I would have said that no single bee has any measure of independence, yet you say that energetically they have. I guess when we study bees from a scientific viewpoint we get one conclusion while from a lifelong bee keeper we would get another. I'll go with the dedicated keeper of bees. Incidentally, when you say . . . with exceptions, I take it you mean those people of a higher consciousness?"

Yes. As you leave the consciousness of the collective beliefs and concepts of life, you are far more free to make an assessment of a situation independent of the forgone and attached conclusions of the collective.

I sigh. "How true. This is the process we are now going through. The collective or mass consciousness is being challenged on a daily basis by the lies and deceit of the few over the many. It is my observation that when you do not fully trust yourself, then you subconsciously trust the mass belief. A sort of *safety in numbers* type of thinking. I consider this now to be a type of imbalanced and/or misleading thinking. Now we should be thinking that if the many believe it, it is likely to be incorrect."

The people in this frame of reality are an incredibly complicated, self-deceiving species.

"I agree, but this too will pass. We will grow up eventually and move along with our own evolution of consciousness."

I smile. "Thank you for the insight into bee communication!

I am planning another journey into the other reality that exists on my little mountain ridge. If you don't mind, I will do this by myself."

I laugh. "Okay, I said that all wrong. Of course you don't mind and I am not asking for your permission. I am ready to revisit the amazing city."

Enjoy . . . but be conscious.

*   *   *

It was about a week later that I prepare myself for the return. I have been constantly nagged by Pan's closing comment, "be conscious." I do my best to be conscious most of the time. Why would he say that out of the blue? Is there something going on that I should know? I have tried asking him, but this is one of the many questions to which I get no reply, no answers.

Pan's odd, seemingly misplaced words, have left me rather disconcerted. To my knowledge, Pan never misplaces his words. His words are meaningful, so what does *"be conscious"* mean? Of course, I know what they mean, but to what context is he applying this? Oh god, I give up!

One sunny morning after a long period of rain, I sit, not quite relaxed, in my study chair. I move consciously through my chakras and into the fifth chamber, and putting far more effort into it than I did previously, I vigorously launch myself metaphysically toward the city, but . . .

* * *

. . . oh, my gosh, where am I?

This time I recognise the area and its familiar contours simply because there is no city to hide the definition of the land. There are no trees, no shrubs, nothing, except for the utter strangeness that confronts me. Imagine the area with hundreds, maybe thousands of white balloons floating on five metre long strings which just brush the green, lawn-like grass beneath them. That's it. No people, no city, no anything except white balloons!

I telepathically call out . . . "Hello. Hello . . . anyone here?"

Nothing . . . !

For a while I just stand, completely nonplussed, utterly disconcerted. What do I do? Finally, I walk among the white balloons to more closely study them. Of course, the strings are not strings; that would be too simple. The strings are very thin, soft, flexible yet tough tubes, each covered in a super fine layer of what appears as very short hair. And as I touch a tube the hair moves, rippling away from my light metaphysical touch. I realise now that what appeared to be hair is a mass of short, very active tendrils.

Okay, so they are alive! Now what?

Floating upward about five metres in my metaphysical body I

am quickly among a cluster of the so-called balloons. Of course, the string is not string, so the balloons will not be balloons! I reach out to very gently and carefully touch one of the balloons. As I do so, it very gently, carefully and skilfully avoids my sensitive metaphysical fingers. This is getting curiouser and curiouser.

Sitting among them in my favourite lotus position, I attempt to engage them telepathically. Very softly I ask, "What are you? Who are you? Where am I?"

I enjoy the lotus position simply because it is no longer possible for me to do this physically. Once, long ago, but not now. My knees do not like it! I have a sense of great delicacy among the balloons, and I intend to make sure that I am sensitive to them, and . . . conscious!

Only silence greets me.

As I look at one that is very close to me, I notice that it, also, is covered in the same short tendrils as the strings, or rather, tubes. As I change my vision, drawing the balloon closer to my eyes/perception, just like the tube, the surface of the balloon ripples. By watching intently, I notice that the tendrils are continually rippling, making the balloon appear slightly hazy, rather than clearly defined. Now, I can see that they are all like this. As I continue to observe them silently, I get the inner feeling that they are also observing me. I can almost feel them relaxing. This is a life form, or life forms completely unknown to me. Closely observing them, I think that I can see the slightest expansion and deflation of the balloons, but it is so slight that I am not sure.

I am aware that although time is passing, equally no time is passing. My humanness is in conflict with the greater metaphysical reality of all time occupying the same moment. Nevertheless, I am okay with this.

Very slowly and subtly, the creatures are moving closer to me. I keep very still as they cluster ever closer.

Finally, I am engulfed in them. Remaining very conscious and aware, I am feeling a brief touch of fear, but I am not sure that it came from me. It passes quickly, but I sense that it came from them.

Gradually I become aware of what feels like a very mild electrical current running through me and over me. It seems to carry a sense of inquiry. I am now aware that the tendrils on them are rippling as though grass in a strong wind. I have the feeling that they are attempting to communicate with me . . . but I don't ripple!

Once again, in my softest inner whisper, I ask, "Who are you? Where am I?"

Is it my imagination, or am I feeling telepathic imprints from them? Not so much flowing words, but impressions that somehow make sense as it translates into my consciousness. *Weee are not of theee.*

We are not of the! Of the what? What does this mean? As I attempt to keep my thoughts to myself, I get a sudden flash of insight. Oh no, my vigorous launch to reach the city has caused this. I only need to focus and step *Between*, but no, I had to over-compensate . . . all because of Pan's *"be conscious"* remark, and my ridiculous reaction to it. By my irregular reaction, I have launched myself into a strange astral realm connected to the city and the people. I think! Or maybe not. Am I being too logical?

How clever of me! Just act normally and all would be well. Now I am in an astral realm that is unlike any that I have previously encountered, and I have encountered some real oddities! Intuitively, I know that I am correct.

"I have no idea what you mean," I telepathically project.

My situation has triggered an old memory. When I was a young boy I used to listen to a radio programme called Twenty Questions. A team of three people would have to guess what the object in question was, and they could only ask twenty questions to get to it. The first question was always; animal, mineral or vegetable.

This is what I am thinking right now as I face this conundrum. I again get the feeling of mental impressions; *weee are none of theesee.*

Hmm . . . if I can trust these impressions, we are communicating. I would have guessed that these things, creatures, whatever, are vegetable, but they sure don't act like them . . . and they are certainly not mineral. And any idea of animal seems to be neither in their energy or forms.

With deliberation, I metaphysically raise myself maybe another ten metres higher, so that I am well above the forest of balloon-creatures. I did wonder if they occupied just the space of my garden, but like the city, they are spread out over a much wider area. Okay, so assuming this is an astral realm, and accepting that nothing is by accident, nothing by chance, why am I here? What do I have to learn, or what do I have to offer?

I can see no deviation in the forest of balloon-creatures. No different colours, all at about the same height, all seemingly aware to some degree, all very mysterious. I definitely need to think outside the box!

Hmm . . . this is interesting. In the area where they clustered around me, about thirty of the balloon-creatures are rising up to my height, about twice the height they were previously. And even more odd, as they rise up their tubes grow longer thus maintaining contact with the earth/grass.

Once again, they cluster around me, but I get the feeling they are not comfortable with this height. So, I rise up about twice as high again. The cluster that had followed me are showing signs of agitation as they once again follow me higher. The thirty or so of them are showing tinges of red in the balloons. I wonder what this means? As I glance downward, their tubes are having trouble maintaining contact with the earth/grass. Some of the tubes are hovering a metre above it, while clearly attempting to grow or stretch themselves longer.

Okay, enough. I seem to be causing them distress as they accompany me, so I move downward back to their original height of around five metres.

Their relief at this is almost palpable. I can feel them somehow relaxing as the thirty follow me down, their tubes retracting and literally caressing the short grass that grows all over. The grass is thin and wiry, looking as though freshly mowed. I had not given that a thought, but how can it grow and remain short if nobody mows it?

Aha . . . they do it. In some way the tubes withdraw energy from the grass, while maintaining its life and height. And animals graze! Are these then some form of astral herbivore?

I get an odd, but stronger impression that I should not attempt to classify them for my own comfort. My comfort? Hmm . . . there is truth to this. With even the most basic classification, I make the unknown more known and familiar. I need to embrace the mystery they represent, rather than attempt to solve it.

Moving down to the grass, I walk among the trailing tubes. I notice that no matter how the balloon-creatures move around, the tubes never seem to cross over one another, or ever get entangled. This time the tubes are far more animated. Some are curling up toward me, so I stand still, allowing them to gently caress my metaphysical body. Interestingly, I can feel their touch on me. I can almost feel their curiosity, as the tubes both caress and probe. I have to accept that there is intelligence here, an awareness that is becoming ever more obvious.

Not only can the tubes extend, but I now see that the tendrils are also extending as they stroke over my metaphysical body. In my reality I have no metaphysical substance when compared with my physical body, but here they are clearly aware of substance as their tendrils explore my Being.

This touching began with the thirty or so more adventurous balloon-creatures, but now there is a large crowd of them with their tubes draped all over me. I choose to allow this, as I feel their harmlessness. I think!

Noticing that the light is very subdued, rather like a normal twilight, I rapidly rise to a position high above the astral creatures, leaving them all behind. It is daytime, so I look for the sun, expecting to see the sun with which I am familiar. It is not here. This sun is three times larger and as pale as our full moon. Okay, this I did not expect. Now I not only do not know what these creatures are, but I have no idea where I am. I seem to have launched myself into a totally different frame of reality.

Back on the grass once more, I am immediately like a magnet to the tubes as they move in their hundreds toward me. There is something very odd about this whole set-up. Although it is subtle, I am gradually feeling drained of energy with all these tubes touching me. It feels rather like an energy-suck. Energy suck! Oh my gosh, just as they feed on the energy of the grass, are they attempting to feed on my energy? It seems so.

I do not like this. I have no foundation on which I can make sense of what is happening here and, quite honestly, neither do I want to embrace the mystery . . . as I so often say! This is one mystery that I will happily leave behind. It's too weird . . . and the longer I stay here it is getting increasingly spooky. So, how do I return when I have no clue where I am? It seems to me that this is going to be all about focus and clarity. I need to focus on my physical body, as this is literally the anchor for my metaphysical body. Not that I like normal under normal circumstances, but right now, normal seems attractive.

It is challenging to quietly focus on my physical body in my study while I am slowly being covered, caressed, and probed by an ever growing number of tendril covered tubes. And now that I am aware of it, I can feel the very subtle drain of energy. I have encountered the occasionally human energy-suck, but these creatures are in a whole different category, plus there are so many of them.

Because I do this often, I am aware of the moment of clarity in my focus, and with no great launching, I carefully step . . . *Between* . . . and back into the familiar safe energy of my physical body in my study.

* * *

Phew . . . I am glad this is finished. I'm not sure that I learned anything other than to not act irrationally at irrational moments!

Nine

A wise mentor allows the student to create their own lessons ... lessons they do not know they need to learn.

"So, what did I learn?" I ask sarcastically.

A whole new approach named 'gently, gently.' You carry a lot of energy, a lot of inner-power. You have no need to hurl yourself into the situations that you so often do. A calm, more gentle and trusting approach has now been accomplished. Your lesson to yourself.

I HAD ARRANGED WITH HENRY to do a video of me talking about my garden as we walked around it. Henry is a very close friend of mine, and since the very beginning of the Forest Garden, he has helped me to both create it and maintain it. There is no money involved, just a close friendship and a shared love of working in the garden. Another close friend, named Bruno, also began to help us, so we dubbed ourselves the Three Amigos. Not very original, I agree, but we have a lot of fun together, are very close, and consume quite a few mugs of cappuccino on a regular weekly basis.

Both Henry and Bruno are best described as semi-retired. Henry has been a man of many talents, and photography is one of them. Although videoing is new to him, he has a natural feel for the way of it. Bruno is a semi-retired Swiss medical doctor who specialises in homeopathy. He is brilliant at this. Although this was popular and acceptable in Switzerland, and indeed much of Europe, it is a struggle in Oz with the AMA discrediting it simply because they do not understand it. I guess it is not scientific enough!

Anyway, they are both financially independent, but both may do occasional jobs. Working with me is probably the most underpaid work on the planet . . . and it is often *hard* work! To round out the picture, while Bruno is now single, Henry is married to the delightful Song Hi Lee. She is a brilliant Intuitive Healer, and an excellent personal masseuse—for us only—along with a quite painful therapy that I describe as tendon-ouch!-realignment. She is also Carolyn's personal yoga coach, fitness trainer and very close friend. To be honest, Carolyn is her spiritual mother of choice!

I need to add that we all have a rather wonderful Love for each other, with full trust and a vulnerability to share from the heart. Personally, I consider a Love such as we share to be a profound blessing.

So it was that one sunny day in a very wet La Nina summer, Henry and I spent one whole morning—after the essential cappuccino, of course—making a video of my garden. It took far longer than I expected, and at the end of two plus hours, we had only videoed the first half. So it was decided that we will have a Part One, The Forest Garden, which is new and developing, and Part Two, The Heart Garden which is very well established. Of course, me being me, I raved a lot about establishing a garden, on and on, in a long and drawn-out video. However, I know perfectly well that by the time it has been edited it will be an appropriate length, and all will be well.

For me, it was a wonderful opportunity to share some of my insights into, and my passion for, gardening. The sheer size of the garden means it is also my never-ending fitness centre.

In a week's time, weather permitting, we will video Part Two, The Heart Garden. And, I have no doubt, my passion will again dominate my good sense, but the editing will bring about balance. Some people have been waiting quite a while for this, and for us it will be a wonderful visual reminder of the developing garden that Carolyn and I can look back on in another twenty or thirty years. By then, the Forest Garden will be fully established and we will find this

Pan . . . and Me

2022 video of its early years almost unbelievable . . . and probably quite comical.

Although I delayed for a while, inevitably I decided it was time to revisit Giles and the sentient city. This time, hopefully, I will arrive in phase, will be expected and met, and be quickly recognised as the blast from the past!

To this end I put in quite a bit of focusing on Giles, on the sentient city, and the whole energy *feeling* of the place. Because of my preparation, I make no huge leap, but rather step carefully and gently . . . *Between* . . . arriving safely in the city.

* * *

Giles is literally waiting for me as I arrive at the same place as my earlier attempt . . . and I am in phase! Happy days!

After the sentient city has greeted me, congratulating me on my safe arrival, Giles and I stroll in the city, chatting together.

"Why did the city congratulate me on my safe arrival?" I ask. "I was safe enough last time, even if a bit out of phase."

Giles frowned. "This is something that I was going to discuss with you. The city and I, and quite a few other people here, felt a powerful disturbance recently, and it seemed to have your energy signature within it."

We are close to a river when a convenient, nearby seat invites us to sit and relax. And I *do* mean it invites us, telepathically, clearly and obviously. To be honest, I am startled, stopping to stare at the seat in surprise.

"Is anything wrong?" Giles asks.

I laugh. "The seat invited us to sit and relax. This simply does not happen in my reality, so I was not expecting it."

"We have a very polite and well-meaning city," Giles smilingly tells me as he makes himself comfortable on the seat. I join him. Hmm . . . very comfortable.

"So, what was this disturbance you mentioned, with my energy signature?"

"I was hoping that you would tell me," he replies.

I feel rather perplexed. "Why would I possibly know anything about what happens here?" I ask him. "You and I live on totally different frequencies."

He smiles. "When I say that this had your energy signature, although it was silent, I liken it to a shout, a loud almost explosive burst of *your* energy. Are you sure that you have not had another misadventure in attempting to reach us?"

"Oh . . . oh my gosh!"

Giles chuckles. "That comment suggests that the mystery is solved."

I tell him in detail about my strange experience with the odd, white balloon looking creatures and their long thin tubes. As I talk about it, he is looking ever more concerned and rather shocked. I remark on this.

"What's the matter? The further I go with my story, the more shocked you seem. I mean, although weird and bizarre, I was perfectly safe."

Giles stares at me wonderingly. "You have no idea, have you?"

"No idea about what? Do you mean the balloon creatures? You're right, I have no clue about where I was or what was going on. Oh, and the sun was huge and pale, with no warmth, even though it was not cold."

Giles gently shakes his head. "How did you get there?"

I laugh. "Okay, the problem began when I told Pan about my intended journey, and he replied that I should *be conscious*. For some reason that threw me. So, me being me, I completely overcompensated and literally launched myself toward this reality . . . and obviously, I missed!"

"And you have no notion of where you were?"

"Not an inkling. I tried to decide if they were animal, mineral or vegetable, and even that did not help. To the best of my cognisance it was an astral realm."

Giles nods emphatically. "Okay, that is the clue I needed to be sure. Would you like to know where you were? I am at a loss as to how you managed to get there, and I will consult with a few friends to verify my thoughts."

"Considering I had already accepted that I will never know, I will be very pleased to find out."

"You jumped into our non-violent version of hell."

"WHAT!"

"As you already know, heaven and hell are both extreme different states of consciousness. We do not have any evil people in our frame of reality, but we do have some who are of a low enough consciousness that they have a dampening effect on the whole. Not a big effect, but it is noticeable," Giles explained.

"What you experienced was the lower astral realm of these people. They are a bit like a parasitic energy-drain to our population rather than being bad, so they get to experience a timeless time while just draining energy." He laughs. "You should have launched yourself into one of our highest astral realms. That would have been a magnificent experience."

I nod pensively. "It all makes sense. After a while I could feel my energy dwindling, and I felt that they may be taking it, but I was not sure. Wow . . . so I went to hell!" I laugh. "That is a very placid version of hell. I can tell you that some of our lower astral realms are seriously horrible, especially the ones related to murder, or the torture and rape of children. Also, the alcohol and drugs related hell is really nasty stuff. Seriously, your hell is very mild by comparison, but I guess it demonstrates the futility of living that way."

I smile at him. "How come you are so familiar with hell? In my reality very few people would have a clue about it"

He laughs. "Overall, we are a conscious and aware people. As I said, none are bad or violent, but a small percentage feeds on the energy of the whole rather than grow in consciousness from their own efforts. We are aware of where they go when they leave their body. Obviously, those who go there did not believe such a place existed, but every cause has its effect."

"I would have thought that you would be beyond cause and effect."

Giles shakes his head. "Make no mistake, we are still growing in consciousness. Many, like myself, experience cause and effect almost simultaneously, but by no means all of us. This reality is not the end of consciously growing. We are all in the same University of Life as you, even if we are in a higher grade."

"It would seem that you do not have the huge diversity of different states of consciousness that we do. We range from purely evil people who would control our world, to sociopathic murderers, to pedophiles, to parasitic scammers, to thugs, to angry and violent people, to liars, to abusing the aged, on and on down the scale toward a lower astral hell," I said.

"But to balance this most people are decent and law abiding. They are caring and generous, quick to rally around families in need, donating both money and goods to charities. We have deeply compassionate people, and people who would probably sacrifice their own life for another. These are the higher consciousness, true saints of our people. They are unknown until that vital moment they are needed . . . and they act."

Giles nods sagely. "No, we have nothing like that amazing diversity. Taking responsibility for yourself and being responsible for our society as a whole features strongly in our people. It is only the very small percentage of energy-drains that must learn that there is a better way."

"We have them too, but they are often the husbands and wives and/or family who are not recognised as such. Only a few are deliberate, by far the most of them are unaware that they drain the energy of the people around them. And, equally, we have those people who have so much energy they are like radiant miniature suns in the lives of the people who know and love them. We truly are a mixed bag," I say with a small laugh.

We sit for a while in reflective silence.

"Can I show you more of the city?" Giles asks.

"Sure, I would like that. Do you have any museums, or cinemas?"

"Cinemas . . . you mean like the old-fashioned movie houses?"

I nod.

"Not as such. There is a passion at the moment for looking back, and even revisiting, our past history so that it can be reenacted not as history wrote it, which was almost invariably inaccurate, but as it most likely actually happened."

"So you make movies of this?"

Giles chuckles. "Oh no, your movies are also our history. We have holographic versions now that are so brilliant you find it difficult to watch and retain a sense of self as the observer, rather than a participant. Rather than looking at it on a screen, you are totally involved in the action all around you."

I laugh. "That sounds a bit scary to me. Imagine a war movie where you are involved. No thanks, not for me."

"I agree. We seldom make such projections. Mostly they are extremely creative and rather beautiful, while being very illuminating. The idea is for entertainment and education. Also, they can be consciousness expanding."

Without warning, I feel a sudden sensation of wanting to return to my own frame of reality. Not a negative feeling at all, but a feeling of being out of place, rather than out of phase. I make no attempt to analyse the how and why of it, I mostly just follow my stronger intuitive feelings. They never let me down.

Explaining all this to Giles, I tell him that I have much to explore on the levels of the various realms of Nature. "Before I go, I would like to thank you for all your many courtesies to me, particularly explaining the odd version of your hell into which I unfortunately projected myself. I think that 'gently, gently' might be my new mode of travel!"

After bidding him and the city fare-well, I gently step . . . *Between* . . . realities and back into my study.

* * *

I sit for a while reflecting on my journey.

Next time, just before a journey, if Pan suggests that I be conscious, I will be conscious of not reacting to the suggestion. Did he know that I would react in such a manner?

I sigh . . . I guess I will never know, but it certainly became a powerful lesson for me.

A couple of days later I had to ask. I just couldn't let it be!

"Pan . . . would you be kind enough to tell me why, when I said that I was planning another journey, you told me to be conscious?"

I inner-feel a chuckle. *You got into all sorts of a pickle over that.*

"Yes, I know, but why that comment?"

A wise mentor allows the student to create their own lessons . . . lessons they do not know they need to learn.

"So, what did I learn exactly?" I ask sarcastically.

A whole new approach named 'gently, gently.' You carry a lot of energy, a lot of inner power. You have no need to hurl yourself into the situations that you so often do. A calm, gentle and trusting approach is now learned. Your lesson to yourself.

"Hmm . . . I have to confess that this is probably a lesson that I needed, but why spring it on me like that?"

I but made a comment, all the rest was self-fabricated.

"Okay, okay, but you could have given me some warning."

A warning . . . for you? Is this a joke? You would have dismissed it.

What can I say? Somehow, I seem to have outsmarted myself!

Ten

Where do <u>you</u> come from, or originate? Your answer is the same as mine. You are life discovering life in a human form with no beginning and no ending. And where are you going in your eternal journey? You have no idea as a human person, and as an expression of Divine Being, the question is meaningless. You are the journey which you are journeying.

In my new Forest Garden, the far above-normal amounts of rain have created more growth this year than the previous three years put together. During our time of La Nina, I have been observing the plant development on our mountain ridge. I often wondered in times of drought, when growth was so minimal, if the rather eroded ridge soil was seriously lacking in the needed elements. Now, with the abundance of water and the amazing plant growth, I realise that the soil is okay. No matter how good or even poor the soil may be, it is the rain and the sun in perfect combination that is the factor of greatest growth. Of course, I am not suggesting that the soil need not have a good humus content, or be badly lacking in soil nutrients, such as the anion and cation minerals and trace elements. Without question, whatever deficiency there is in the nutrients of the soil, the plants will also be lacking.

Having decided to focus on the various unseen realms of Nature when I do more metaphysical travelling, I was sitting in my study one overcast, drizzling day, looking out the window. Dreary, I thought. Just like an average gloomy weather day in England; overcast, without any *real* rain. Gosh, the days I remember like that. Too much cloud and drizzly rain and nowhere near enough sun seemed to be the pattern of my youth. And then in 1947 when I was ten years old, we had month after month of hot sun. I got so badly sunburnt, along with sunstroke, it almost killed me! I was bedridden for many weeks and very sick. That was my first flirtation with death. I had no idea then that death and I would cross paths often . . . and in such stupid ways. I was foolishly unconcerned and negligent with my wellbeing as a youth, and even into my twenties. I paid quite a price for my self-neglect.

Happily, that is all in my distant past.

Now, sitting in my study, I relax, shifting my focus from contemplating my memories, toward my metaphysical body. It is time to do some more metaphysical adventuring in my same mountain ridge home space but on a different frequency . . . which is, literally, an entirely different realm of reality.

With no fuss or bother, I gently step metaphysically . . . Between . . . emerging into a very different and startling reality.

* * *

How is this possible?

I live on a mountain ridge. But now I am standing in my metaphysical body on the bank of a wide river. Wow, talk about a different reality realm occupying the same space! Even though I thought I am prepared for the differences, it still catches me by surprise.

The sun is shining, and there is a pervading energy of peace and clarity. I smile in delight. This is nothing like I expected, although after my previous fiasco with over-jumping, I did not know what to expect. This, however, is incredible! How this can be in the same space, even if on a higher frequency, is a complete mystery to me? As a metaphor, it is a bit like seeing a rainbow with its different colours of the spectrum, knowing all contribute to that one delightful display . . . and yet, being surprised. Of course, we only see the colours that have a frequency slower than the speed of light. Seldom do people ever speculate on the higher, unnamed frequency colours that we are unable to see with our physical eyes. Obviously, the same analogy can be applied to what we describe as physical reality.

Gazing across the river I am impressed by its clarity. The water is flowing with a medium-strong current, and it seems that nothing impairs its clarity and purity. Peering into its depths, I can see shapes and shadows sliding gently along, some moving against the current, others flowing with it. It is all so effortless, whether with the current or against it.

When you are in the true flow of life, all is effortless. There is no with or against. There is only flow and its accompanying lucidity.

I look around to see where the telepathic words are coming from, but I see nothing but the river and the huge meadow of wild grasses through which it flows. Silently, I agree.

While looking for the speaker, I see something floating across the river toward me. It looks like a huge leaf! Amazingly, it is flowing directly across the current, completely unaffected by it. As it draws closer, I see that it looks like a huge leaf from a massive water lily. In a botanical hothouse I have seen the floating leaves of the world's largest water lily (Victoria amazonica) with their curled-up leaf edges. A real giant among water lilies, their leaves can be up to 3 metres in diameter, and may be carried on a stem that is over 7 metres in length. This one, although not any bigger, is a far stronger, more robust leaf, making ours appear frail by comparison.

Obviously moving with intent and purpose, the huge leaf floats directly toward me, so I wait for its arrival.

Intent and purpose will enable you to easily ride on the varying currents of life. A clear focus is lacking in many of your kind, thus they drift half afloat and half submerged in the river of life.

Although I do not recognise the energy of the telepathic words, I smile. Hmm . . . a very philosophical lily leaf. This is my unspoken thought.

Is it not your intent and purpose to assist people such as I mention? Is it not your intent and teaching that Truth will uplift you while the weight of fear will drag you down?

Okay, this leaf has my full attention!

"Are you reading my thoughts?"

Not really. I am responding to the full coverage broadcast of your thoughts and their accompanying emotions.

I sigh. "Sorry. I thought I had shut that down, but obviously it is not yet automatic. Thank you for drawing my attention to this."

By now the huge leaf is sitting calmly on the water surface close to me. It looks big and sturdy enough to even support a couple of physical people. The edges curl up quite high, looking very strong and capable.

I wait for the obvious request to hop in.

This is your choice, my friend, but if you are aware of the obviousness of the request, why do you wait? Do you need validation, or permission?

I feel perplexed. Obviously, this leaf knows my every thought, but by the tone of its telepathic energy I feel as though I am being examined . . . and found wanting.

"Yes, in my world, we do wait for an invitation. To simply jump aboard would be both presumptuous and rude."

Fair enough. It is very rarely that I ever make a connection with a human from your realm. I apologise if I was rude.

"You are not so much rude, as blunt."

Do we not then share the same quality?

I laugh. "While I may not agree with you, I'm sure some people would."

To avoid further issues, I carefully step into and onto the giant leaf. I am aware already of having substance in this realm, even if it is metaphysical substance, so I feel a touch of apprehension. However, the leaf feels as similar and solid to me as if it were a physical wood boat in my physical realm.

You can trust in the integrity of my structure.

"I do . . . absolutely. But could you tell me the purpose of this? I would also like to know how a single giant water lily leaf can be sentient. Also, if we are going on a journey, I would like to know where we are going, and why?"

So many questions.

"Reasonable ones, surely."

Did you come on this journey to question or to experience?

If this is what it is like to dialogue with me when I am in a blunt mood, I can now understand why I may ruffle a few feathers!

"I came to experience, but the experience has greater value if I am able to comprehend the content of my experience."

Distant laughter echoes across the river.

Clearly it did not come from the lily leaf, but I cannot see any other Beings in our vicinity. Okay . . . what is going on?

The laughter, which is definitely not human, continues on a higher note. It is a lyrical laughter, as though the wind, combined with the twisting leaves of a huge tree, is blowing through the strings of some unearthly cosmic harp.

Strangely, I feel a sudden connection, followed by an unveiling insight.

"The World River," I gasp! "But I don't see how this is possible."

Then we can be very happy that our wondrous realm is not limited by your inability to grasp obvious possibilities.

"You are definitely the most brash and brusque leaf that ever, or never, grew from a plant," I reply.

The laughter drops into a warm and mellow chuckle.

With a sigh, and feeling rather set-up, I await whatever may happen.

Previously when you journeyed with me, I showed you a probability future that you and others of your kind would enjoy.

"Yes, I remember. I understand that although it is a probability for me, it is a reality for those who are within that frequency realm. Am I correct?"

Yes, you are correct. Oh . . . and please do not be upset with the leaf. This is but the boatman I have sent for you. All your dialogue is with me. Just as you have humour, so also do I, or we, or us, or consciousness.

"Really! Consciousness has humour? With the greatest respect, that seems unlikely enough to be impossible. How can consciousness possibly have humour?"

Are you suggesting that humanity invented humour?

"No, of course not . . . but . . . but . . !"

But this is what you thought, yes! You have seen animals and birds clearly playing, yet have you not heard their sounds of laughter? Dogs with joyful barking and parrots and magpies chortling are just a couple of examples. Did you not hear the river you sat with while you learned to listen? Yes, it spoke to you, but it also laughed at you and with you. Have you not heard the trees chuckling in the rain after a long dry spell? Or the delighted sounds of the soil as it receives new moisture? And are all these separate entities in Nature? Or is it possible that the consciousness of All life expresses humour in life forms beyond that of just humanity?

"Hmm . . . well that puts me in my place! Obviously I am wrong in my somewhat arrogant speculation. I have definitely seen dogs laughing with their facial expressions and sounds, but it never occurred to me that they share a sense of humour with us. As for the trees and soil, yes, in my deeper moments I have been aware of this on a metaphysical level, but you are showing me that complacency is easily developed and not so easily lost. I heard the river laugh often during those years it was teaching me, but even within all that, I still failed to associate humour and laughter as universal in consciousness. I am sincerely grateful. Thank you for this insight."

Suddenly, I feel a wave of Love moving through me.

Child, know that you are an extraordinary human. You stand here in realms that are unknown to most of your kind, and we marvel at your ability. Despite this, you have a true humility and openness to learn ever more.

Come, journey with me as I open a new world to you, and for you.

The words almost explode from me. "But why me? There are so many brilliant people who would understand far more of what you reveal, than me. I am comparatively uneducated."

You are the alchemy that connects. It is not brainpower or education, but the dynamic of compatible energy, and this you possess in abundance. You are not a personalised selection by us. It is the alchemy in your field of energy in its synchronisation within the metaphysical realms of life.

I sigh deeply in relief. Wonderful. I have long carried a tiny anxiety that in some weird way I am the wrong person in some crazy cosmic mix-up. This is why the World River's words are so refreshingly wonderful for me. Pan has occasionally reassured me of this, but . . . I guess I needed more! Now, I am aware that the long-held anxiety is rapidly fading.

Standing within the structure of the leaf, I feel reassured on several levels. As I connect with it, I feel its laughter. A leaf . . . with humour! Okay, embrace it.

"Where are we going?" I ask, immediately feeling foolish. I mean, in my realm this makes sense . . . but here . . . is there a where?

"I know that you are the World River, but where do you come from, or originate, and where do you flow to?" I ask.

Where do you come from, or originate? Your answer is the same as mine. You are life discovering life in a human form with no beginning and no ending. And where are you going in your eternal journey? You have no idea as a human person, and as an expression of Divine Being, the question is meaningless. You are the journey which you are journeying.

I sigh. And I thought that Pan was the riddle specialist.

The strange melodic all-embracing laughter peals out not so much as sound, but more as a joyful feeling.

Okay, I am still inadvertently telepathically broadcasting my thoughts.

Time to focus.

As I look around me, I see that we have floated across the surface of the current toward the middle of the river. As before, I am aware that although to me this looks very similar to physical water, it is more an unknown liquid energy. It is an amazing river of flowing energy that has liquid qualities without necessarily being a liquid . . . if that even makes sense!

Consider me/us as a meridian flow of universal energy. I am endless flow of eternal energy. I connect all life in ways unknown to your humanity. In reality realms of a higher consciousness, I am recognised and known, even while I remain as Mystery. Just as your Earth has ley lines, which are meridian flows of energy, so does your physical and metaphysical bodies. The meridian lines of your immortal metaphysical body are far more powerful than those of the temporary and mortal physical body . . . as would be expected.

"Does this mean that I make such a strong connection with you because I am here metaphysically? Sort of flow meets and connects with flow."

I feel an inner acknowledgement. *This is a reasonable metaphor.*

"At our last encounter you told me that you consciously connect the stars in our solar system and in our galaxy. Surely that connection would require a much bigger energetic flow than this aspect of the World River on which I am now floating."

You are correct. You could liken this to a tributary of the main body of the World River I am, but of course, all tributaries are One with me.

"Are there many tributaries?"

Numbers beyond count . . . and all One.

"Yes, I get that. But when I think of the immensity of you as a meridian flow of energy connecting everything in our galaxy to the consciousness of One . . . the mind boggles!"

You are quite unique as a human in that you accept easily without the need to fully understand. This is wisdom.

"I learned long ago that rather than continually struggle to understand, it was more productive to rely on my mystical cognition to reveal the bigger picture in perfect timing for me. I am sure that timing is the key factor."

I repeat . . . this is wisdom.

I feel an inner warmth with these words. I struggled for so long to understand the—for me—non-understandable, before surrendering to a greater inner-knowing that is carried on the wings of a higher level of cognition. We all have this, but the intellect is inclined to fight our higher cognition, rather than cooperate with it. This, along with the mystical nature of higher cognition, and you have an insight into the conflict between the logic of the intellect and the sheer mystery of this higher potential.

And it *is* higher!

During our conversation the leaf has floated me across the World River and I am now approaching the distant bank. Oh my gosh . . . this is as different from the wild meadow as is possible. On this side it appears that the river flows through, or into, a desert.

The leaf stops against a sloping beach of sand and pebbles, making it very easy to step out and walk up the shingle-like strata. All around me it appears to be a dull reddish colour, somehow very alien in appearance. On our physical Earth, rocks vary in colour and formation from country to country, yet they all feel very much like our Earth rocks, or boulders. This place has a very different energy-feeling.

A chill sweeps through my metaphysical body. The energy here is like nothing I have ever encountered. And with the chill comes a deep insight.

Oh my God! I'm on Mars! This can't be possible.

I stop in my tracks. This is not a good idea. Turning around quickly and smoothly, I make a dash for the river and the leaf boat . . . only to abruptly stop. The river has gone, taking the leaf boat with it. In fact, there is nothing to suggest that there ever was a river here. No river bed . . . just desert. Oh my gosh . . . I'm stranded . . . on Mars?!

For a long moment the chill intensifies and I am paralysed by shock and indecision. But as I straighten my stance, my inner disturbance quickly fades, and I feel calm and centred once more. I smile as I remind myself of my immortality.

Well done. I/we are impressed. You recognised or intuited where you are more quickly than expected, and with the shock of this you have recovered your equilibrium very rapidly. It was expected that the shock would rapidly return you to your physical body.

"I could feel myself wavering, but shock is not necessarily fear. I feel no fear, and no need to seek safety. I think the moment of greatest shock was the fleeting thought that I am stranded alone on Mars."

Dear child, you are anything but alone, or stranded . . . as you will soon discover.

Hmm . . . I wonder what this means?

A glance reveals that the river and the boat are not coming back, so with this thought I head further into the desert. Reddish, pinkish, ochre's, even a vague purplish seems to be the dominant colour of the rocks that are around me. On Earth, our rocks are a wide range of colour from ochres to grey and almost black/brown as the dominant colours. On Earth the rock colour goes right through, but here I get the strange impression that the larger rocks around me are wrapped in colour, rather than fully being that colour. Weird! Maybe it's just me!

There is no path to follow, but a thick dust among the stones and rocks is evident. I smile . . . obviously it has not rained lately! Because I am here in my metaphysical body, I cause no more disturbance on the surface than would a shadow. Happily, I have no need to breathe in my non-physical body, otherwise I would be in serious trouble. I sigh . . . the little I have read about the red planet offers me no help.

What boggles me is how easily the World River duped me and dumped me here. It was certainly not what I had in mind when I began this adventure!

I sigh. This is so typically me.

From my mountain ridge to Mars in one easy step. Who would have even considered it? Or thought it possible? I wonder . . . is there any physical or metaphysical connection between my rocky mountain ridge and this rocky planet? Plenty of new questions, but no answers. Okay, I'm good with this. Ah, an idea.

"Pan . . . are you by any chance in the neighbourhood? This would be a good time to be with me. PAN, CAN YOU HEAR ME?"

Nothing. Not even a distant chuckle. I have had enough metaphysical experience to know that I am not abandoned, but a bit of company right now would be very welcome.

As if my thought was a summons, I am suddenly aware of a strange figure walking/floating alongside me. As I notice him/her/it, the figure turns and, sort of, smiles at me.

I stop in astonishment and stare at the figure.

The figure stops and regards me, still sort of energetically smiling.

The Being I am looking at is not quite as tall as me in my metaphysical body, which energetically is about five times larger than my physical body. So, this Being is very tall, with an impression of being very thin. The figure is wearing a long robe, from neck to almost sweeping the ground. Even as I look, I get a strange, but unsubstantiated impression that there is nothing inside the robe, and that it is for my benefit only. The head and face on the upright figure are equally strange. The head is completely bald, while a flexible mask seems to cover the face. Or is it a false layer of skin? Whatever it is, I have no idea if it is real and covering a hidden face, or if it is an actual, almost fully protected face. The eyes, however, appear to be normal except for colour. They are a vividly bright gold. No ears are evident, and not much more than a generous slit for a mouth. I get the impression that the ears and mouth are not very important, or are unnecessary.

Does my appearance disturb you?

"Er . . . no, not really. I have met many metaphysical Beings that look so totally bizarre to me, that you are not disturbing. Your sudden appearance, however, was a shock. Er . . . !"

With that strange half hidden half smile, the Being says, *You have a lot of questions . . . yes?*

"I have so many I don't know where to begin."

Allow me to explain myself to some degree. The very fact that you, as a metaphysical human, are on the planet you know as Mars indicates that you are aware of and familiar with metaphysical and multidimensional reality.

"Yes, I am."

So, it should be of no surprise to you that I, and my kind live here, even if temporarily.

I smile. "Only to the extent that our human knowledge suggests that Mars has little to no atmosphere and therefor has no life. Beyond, possibly, bacteria. Of course, this means physical, biological 3-dimensional life as we of humanity know and experience it."

We live some distance from here, so let us quickly finish our journey.

So saying, the Being turns and stares into my eyes. The vivid gold flashes briefly, and I have the sense of gentle, very slow, yet incredibly rapid movement, and as I look around, the whole landscape has changed.

"Oh my gosh!"

I am standing in a very beautiful valley filled with lush vegetation. I need to quickly add that although lush, it is a range of reddish, pinkish colours, not our familiar green. I find it a tad disconcerting at first, but why? It is only a different colour.

"Wow . . . this is different."

Allow me to continue. I and my kind are Beings of a higher dimension, as is this valley. Even atmosphere is affected by dimensional differences. For you physically, where we stand would be a quick death, yet in this dimension life thrives, just as metaphysically you also do so.

"Is it only this valley that has a higher dimension?"

No, all Mars has multiple dimensions, just as Earth does. This valley is special in that it has been landscaped for our pleasure and food. We have a small amount of water here, also of a higher frequency/dimension. On a higher dimension all Mars has vegetation, but it is not so vigorous or so pleasing to our senses as in this valley. We are not a prolific people, and as you already discern, all is not quite as it appears.

Reaching out I attempt to touch a plant and I am surprised that I can feel its texture. This suggests that the vegetation is on my metaphysical wave length. Despite this, I suspect that the Being is on an altogether higher energetic bandwidth.

"Why do I get the impression that there is no body . . . or, no body density under your robe? Do you even have a body?"

The Being shrugs and the robe falls away. As I suspected, there is nothing of substance beneath it, but I can discern a . . . blur, or haze, of coiling, writhing energy that is in the approximate shape of a humanoid body.

We did not wish to cause you distress, so the robe is a curtesy and no trouble to us.

As he telepathically communicates to me, his face is also changing. The mask, or false covering is fading, while a face that seems skinless is slowly emerging. To be honest, it is a shockingly confronting face because we are so used to skin. I am looking at a skinless face that is without blood yet is of a higher frequency that appears to be a continual, gently writhing movement of almost transparent fluid energy. It is seriously difficult to explain simply because it does not exist in our reality. The only comfortable continuity is the golden eyes.

Even though metaphysically I do not breathe, I metaphorically take a deep breath to steady my nerves. Seriously weird . . . this Being's face could be seen as both demonic or angelic. Yet although I can see both points of view as valid, the face to me is in the angelic spectrum.

"I'm sorry if I seem to be rude, but you are nothing like any Being I have ever encountered."

On the contrary, I did not expect to be able to reveal myself to you at all. It was your calm and easy acceptance of me that enabled me to . . . take the risk! I know of your human species aversion to alien visages. You are a very isolated and sheltered species.

Staring at the faint writhing movement in the features before me, I struggle to suppress a shudder. It is as though bloodless veins and arteries are in endless subtle movement, and with no skin cover the movement is both fascinating and appalling. Sheltered as a species is a completely inadequate description of us. If or when we encounter the grotesque, we are threatened. Although I am not threatened by the Being's appearance . . . I am certainly very challenged. And to be honest, it is not grotesque at all . . . just very different.

Happily, I am recovering fast.

"Although you said that you are a visitor, was this once your home planet? Like when it had an atmosphere?"

I confess I was thinking about the planned Mars landings in our future, and wondering what the astronauts would do if confronted by such Beings. A tiny cynical part of me speculated they would shoot first and ask questions later . . . or just freak out and head for home!

No more than Earth is the home planet of humanity.

"There are many people who would challenge that statement."

But you are not one of them.

It was a statement, not a question.

"No, it has been our classroom for a very long time . . . too long, far too prolonged, but some of us keep on moving along. We are going through end-of-term examinations and evaluation right now, and once again a minority will ascend to higher levels of human expression. The majority will have to repeat the term . . . but that's okay. It is as it is. However, I suspect that it is likely you know far more about Earth and humanity than I do.

"Would I be correct in assuming that you are a 6-dimensional Being? And forgive me if I am rude, but do you have a name and are you male or female?"

The Being smiles, or at least, this is my assessment of the alarming movement in its features.

My name cannot be pronounced, it is a unique energetic expression. However, in my experience of humanity, the name Xeeth is close enough and is pronounceable.. And, although we do not have males and females as in humanity, my energy although well balanced, is more inclined toward the masculine in expression.

"Thank you . . . Xeeth. How about your dimension?"

As you have discovered, there is more to this than just dimensions. You humans have many levels of 3-dimensional reality, and those dimensions are inclined to have varying densities. The best I can translate for you is that I am indeed, a 6-dimensional Being of eighth level density. However, for you, now, I am projecting in fourth level density so that we are able to connect more easily.

"I understand . . . I think! I know enough about the levels of density in humanity to interpret your meaning."

I look around me at the beauty in the valley.

"Is the valley a projection from you or am I seeing it in a density that is appropriate to my proclivities?"

Xeeth makes a strange sound. I think it could be a chuckle!

This is a very insightful question. As you surmise, it is appropriate.

"I have a feeling that you are reasonably familiar with humanity, or you know about us. But you are a complete enigma to me. Could you please share something about yourselves with me?"

Eleven

Imagine an enormous pyramid completely inverted, the point downward, the base at the top. This is the situation we all face. The inverted base represents a much higher frequency of life throughout the galaxy, while the lower tip of the pyramid represents the lower, more dense frequency of humanity on Earth. On the larger, higher, finer part of the pyramid, incredible changes have taken place, changes that are totally necessary for the evolution of life to continue in this sector of the universe. This is not just a human problem, this is galactic in scope and scale, involving thousands of different species and races of Beings.

*O*F COURSE, *but first let me show you around.*
Together, we smoothly walk/glide in the direction that he indicates. A shoulder high shrub covered in pinkish flowers is growing close by and it seems vaguely familiar to me. As I think this, I realise that I am attempting to make a connection between these plants and my garden plants, maybe looking for some personal comfort in the familiar. As I examine it closer, all familiarity ends. Our plants put their roots well and truly into the soil for nourishment, water and anchorage. This shrub has a small, yet thick network of roots spread out on the surface of the ground, and even as I watch, it is very slowly moving sideways in tiny, subtle, root movements.

Okay . . . that's different!

Xeeth notices my obvious surprise as I step back. *It should be obvious that plants here are far more evolved than Earth plants in your timeframe. Mars soil is very low in nutrients, so the plants move slowly over the surface transmuting various minerals and soil particles into acceptable nutrients for their wellbeing and growth.*

"Amazing . . . do they need water . . . or air?"

Again, his strange chuckle. *Like us, they create their own moisture.*

I am flabbergasted. "I don't even understand how these plants can be here. Mars is without oxygen, surely. How do they breathe? Creating their own moisture I can just about comprehend, but breathing!?"

Your confusion is understandable as you are used to Earth-type plants. But surely you do not think that all plants follow Earth-bound biological rules.

"Hmm . . . when you put it like that, I have to agree. Are these native to Mars, or were they brought here?"

We brought them here long ago. There are many planets without oxygen but despite this, these plants thrive. Why not here?

Why not, indeed! "I still find it amazing that you create your own moisture. How can you possibly do that? You mean that you do not drink? Do you eat, breathe?"

I pause. "Er . . . sorry, but you really do surprise me. It is difficult to wrench the mind away from what is normal and necessary for humans . . . and most probably not at all normal or necessary for your kind."

As I become more used to Xeeth, I learn to recognise his chuckle, his smile and so on. Certainly it causes facial changes that are mildly disturbing, but his visage seems softer to me now. It is more like moving energy around those golden eyes than a face. It is the eyes that allow for my connection with him. The self-created threat of difference is fading away. Maybe this is why his visage seems to get more natural by the moment. The smile that precedes his easy flowing telepathic communication now seems almost normal.

I did say that we are sixth dimensional Beings. Although I mentioned some plants provide us with food, it is not a necessity for us. Food is pleasurable and, like with your people, a nice social connection.

We do not breathe in the way that you do, but we do have an energetic relationship with the atmosphere we are in. In this way, we synthesise moisture as or when necessary for our wellbeing. To say we take in water would be a huge and misleading overstatement, for our moisture requirements are approximately a large spoon of water within our bodies.

It's my turn to chuckle at myself. This different is very different!

Even the sun seems different! The very reddish sun, which so far has been unrelenting, seems unlike the sun seen from Earth. Here, it is far more hazy, undefined, as though it is shining through a cloud, yet there are no clouds. Maybe it shines through airborne particles? Paradoxically, it seems much closer and yet further away!

As we move quite quickly around the valley, neither of us walking with legs, but simply gliding along on what feels like a cushion of air . . . but obviously is not . . . I think! . . . we share an enjoyable silence. I have let go of my endless questions simply because they accomplish so little. Embrace the mystery, this works. Exploring the differences simply makes me more and more uncomfortable, besides being totally pointless. All I am left with is the possibility of impossibilities! I see numerous other Beings of his kind, but after a glance at us . . . I think . . . they then continue with whatever it is they were doing. Having said that, none of them appear to be doing anything. We are always *doing to* . . . we call it work, maybe sport or gardening or building, whatever. To me, these 'folks' seem much more involved in *being with*, without the need to necessarily be *doing to*.

I am sorry if this sounds like a ramble, but our whole structure of thought and speculation simply does not apply here. I feel rather like a kindergarten boy who is suddenly elevated to high school . . . with no explanation. Over the years of my metaphysical travel, I have accumulated a considerable amount of mystical experience, and it is this that allows me to calmly accept the apparently impossible. I have already learned that in a greater reality, wonders abound!

Obviously I am an open book to Xeeth.

I /we are continually surprised by your lack of strong emotional reactions. *You accept and assimilate with great resilience. If some of us here were to be plunged into your world reality, it is doubtful we would survive it. The shock would be too great.*

"Hmm . . . I never thought about it like that."

Nor have you asked why you have been brought here. He smiles. *It is obviously no accident you washed up on our shores!*

He seems to hesitate over something.

"Is anything bothering you?"

We are Beings with no secrets between us. All is known collectively. You come from a species filled with secrets, words unspoken, things unsaid. You constantly deceive each other on both mental and emotional levels, while we are unable to do this. How comfortable are you with complete open honesty?

I wonder what he is going to tell me. "I prefer it that way."

You are not the first metaphysical traveller that we have brought here. He pauses. *Very briefly, their experiences with us, and of us, were nothing short of disastrous. You are the fifth. The previous travellers ended up almost psychotic. We had to act quickly and metaphysically sedate them.*

I sigh. "That does not surprise me, although I am somewhat surprised that there have been others here before me. Were their travels induced by drugs, or perhaps they were in an astral state? Or were they like me, awake and aware and conscious of their actions?"

You are very aware, very conscious. Let's simply say they were not.

"I had no idea that there is such a thing as metaphysical sedation!"

He chuckles. *You have probably never needed it.*

"Okay . . . so now for the big unasked question. Why <u>am</u> I here?

Just as I am learning to recognise a smile on his visage, so I am now learning to discern when he looks serious. I am beginning to see his face less as strange and alien, more and more as gently moving energy. I am aware that to physical vision he would be completely invisible. The sheer difference of a Being like Xeeth compels me to become cognisant of how much I/we rely on the facial expression of the person or people we are talking to in a conversation. The facial expression tells us of approval or disapproval, trust or lack of it, enthusiasm, interest or boredom, etc., etc. These are markers we subconsciously use to determine how well we are communicating . . . all unrealised. They determine the directions we take in trying to convince or dissuade, either moving toward more humour or to take a serious approach.

For me, now, there is no real facial expression, but there is an energetic link between us that serves in a similar manner. On a very subtle level, his energy conveys humour, intent, seriousness, etc., and I am becoming ever more aware of, and familiar with this.

Xeeth regards me steadily for a few moments. I get the feeling that he is seeing into me and maybe through me. Ah well, I'm an open book to Beings such as these!

With each person we have brought here there was a purpose. Each had the potential we were looking for, but the strangeness overwhelmed them. All is good. None were harmed and none remember. You also hold that potential, although it is a different potential. They were all far more scientifically inclined and trained. However, with or despite all their knowledge, they were not able to reconcile our comparative strangeness, or the situation.

"Hmm . . . I saw you as very strange initially, but quickly saw you as different. I have experienced both strange and different many times."

You are not scientifically inclined. Your approach to life is more simplistic and holistic. This means more balanced. This affects your communication to others and your whole outlook on life. You also have a higher frequency than most, with a greater depth of perception, yet your view of life cannot be shared in scientific terminology. Unfortunately, this is the basic requirement of the mass consciousness. You call it education! This means that much of what you write and speak about is dismissed. You are more a man of the future than a man of the times. What you communicate is deeply appreciated by the few, yet paradoxically, those who need it the most are the least likely to receive it.

I inner-listen in relative silence. This is certainly not the answer

I was expecting. It seems that I come up short of their requirements, whatever they may be. But as a brief summary, I can only agree with him.

"So now the World River will come flowing past and I can return to my own timeframe. Thank you, I have very much enjoyed my visit."

Xeeth chuckles. *Oh no, my dear friend. No river is about to pick you up to return you to your timeframe. In the time you have spent with us, all of us have been examining your energy-field, plumbing the depths of your inner potential, and becoming ever more surprised and pleased with what we find. You correctly surmised that we were 'being with' but you did not realise that it is you we were being with.*

I sigh. "Okay . . . so back to my question. Why am I here?

This I will answer in the fullness of no-time.

I smile and Xeeth chuckles. Amazingly, we share a sense of humour!

Please do not get the impression that we find you lesser than we hoped for. The reverse is true. We find you considerably more than we hoped for. We were looking for scientific understanding, but in you we find cognition and insight of a higher order. This works even better for our purpose. We are also very pleased that my/our honesty in sharing with you has not caused any negative reactions. We are literally unable to lie or deceive.

"I wish the same could be said of us. Our world leaders and global governments are all masters of lies, deception, and corruption."

Yes, so we observe . . . and this brings us to the issue at hand.

During our telepathic conversation we have been walking around the large area of garden, although a vegetated area of beautiful but strange plants might be a better description. Now we are in a section of what appear to be tall and colourful tents. Imagine subtle and mellow rainbow coloured tents of unknown material . . . if material it is!

Xeeth indicates to me to enter the tent before us, and we do so. Although extremes of heat and cold are very subtle experiences for me in my metaphysical body, I am aware of a different, almost effervescent energy in here. It feels very nice. A bit like metaphysically experiencing a fizzy drink throughout your whole body!

Relax, my friend. Just relax. We have much to discuss.

I have an intuitive knowing that if I relax here it will be a very different and comfortable experience. I do so. Of its own volition, my metaphysical body moves into a relaxed and seated position of incredible comfort, yet there is no luxury chair to support me that I can see. Super neat! Although metaphysical fatigue for me is a rare and somewhat unpleasant experience, this no-chair offers a state of inner metaphysical relaxation that is truly wonderful.

I sigh in utter contentment. Like my host, metaphysically I have no need of food or drink so in this no-chair experience, I find a whole new level of relaxation. Relaxed yet alert, my host stands, or hovers before me. Although not strictly necessary, eye contact adds emphasis and energy to telepathic communication, even if one of us is in a metaphysical body. I intuitively know this is why Xeeth is facing me in this way. He has my full attention.

As you may have surmised, we are aware of the energetic global adjustment taking place on Earth. This event is primarily about humanity. Unfortunately, humanity is having a negative affect on Earth, so this adjustment will have a positive affect.

Mars is not our home. This is merely a staging post as we observe the dynamic Changes that are ripping and shredding the old, outmoded human consciousness. There are . . .

I laugh softly, cutting him off. "You mean that we have finally reached our 'use-by' date!"

Energetically, I feel the puzzlement in Xeeth. Before he can ask, I tell him it's just a joke; my irrepressible, sometimes sorry sense of humour.

He regards me for a moment. *And you think we are strange, different.*

I nod. "I admit, I have never encountered any species with a human sense of humour. It is unique in its inappropriateness, its often shockingly bad taste and timing, sometimes cynical, other times sympathetic, and all the other seriously 'off' reasons that we so enjoy about it! However, I do apologise for the interruption. Please continue."

I was about to say that there are many other planetary species with a delegation on Mars at this time. All here to observe humanity in this dynamic of change and to add our considerable energy to the harmonics of the situation. You could also say that we are here to orchestrate the change for the greatest possible good of all.

As I think of the fear, anger, warfare, and confusion raging through so much of humanity in so many countries, I am aware of how a much needed counter balance and guiding influence from a higher level of consciousness would benefit us.

"This assumes that humanity is important in the great scheme of life."

Imagine an enormous pyramid completely inverted, the point downward, the base at the top. This is the situation we all face. The inverted base represents a much higher frequency of life throughout the galaxy, while the lower tip of the pyramid represents the lower, more dense frequency of humanity on Earth. On the larger, higher finer part of the pyramid incredible changes have taken place, changes that are totally necessary for the conscious evolution of life to continue in this sector of the universe. This is not just a human problem, this is galactic in scope and scale, involving many different species and races of Beings.

The lower, denser aspect of the pyramid of life is now going through similar changes. However, in this lower aspect there is huge resistance to change as, despite all the opposition, a global attempt to enslave humanity is being forced toward its completion.

This is the current human situation of Earth. Beyond Earth, humanity is free. It immediately becomes obvious by your energy that you are aware and familiar with what is taking place on Earth. We are resisting this enslavement on powerful energetic levels. Please be aware that everything is energy. The planned enslavement is all about energy; a low energy of deprivation. Your people physically fight for freedom, yet in this way they empower the enemy they resist. This utter futility has continued for too long. We oppose them by counteracting our energy against theirs on a higher, more creative level.

I nod. "Yes, I am aware of what is taking place, so are very many people, but nevertheless, we are the few. To enslave a human you do not need to capture the body, you enslave the mind. Over a long period of time you gradually condition the mind into a form of unwitting compliance. Unrealised, the person becomes submissive, deferring to what they perceive as authority. Today, probably two thirds of humanity has this compliance. This is my guesstimate! Even more interesting, if these people are well developed intellectually, are well educated, and have a deep belief in science, they are somehow even more susceptible to the coercion. They will argue, even fight to prove that they are right and people like me are crazy conspirators. So . . . anything you or other more advanced Beings can do to assist us is more than welcome."

Galactic law does not allow us to directly intervene, but there is nothing to prevent us helping on an energetic level.

"So why doesn't galactic law prevent the direct interference of the lower class of the reptilians, or the lower class of the Greys, or any of the other high tech/low energy Beings that are working with our global elite to enslave humanity?"

Xeeth makes a sound that is almost identical to a deep sigh! *They have been going against galactic law for a very long time. And in this time of galactic change, they, too, will reap what they have sown. This is inevitable. As you correctly surmise, they have a high technology but they are of the lower consciousness of their species. You also have people of a higher and lower consciousness. In the species at the top of this inverted pyramid, the higher consciousness is dominant, so those who act against your welfare are the few, whereas in humanity the lower consciousness is dominant. Those whom you describe as the global elite have a particularly low consciousness, along with dark knowledge and an almost incomparable ruthlessness. They have high tech, vast wealth, and a desire to gain total dominance over humanity. This means the global elite draws from the consciousness of the many, whether willing or not, to energise their bid for total control. If a higher consciousness was dominant in humanity as it is among the more advanced galactic races, then what they are attempting would not be possible.*

I nod. "Although I knew quite a bit of this, I did not know about the differences in consciousness between we humans and other galactic species. That throws a whole new light on things. It's a shock to learn that the overall lower human consciousness is the fuel used to drive their own enslavement. When you explain this, it does make a type of abhorrent sense that I never before realised. The dominant low consciousness is One consciousness, regardless of whether the people as individuals are inclined toward good or bad. Without any judgement, low is low, so to speak."

Yes, this is why consciousness is splitting apart, away from the single great flow of One into multiple flows of One.

I smile. "I get it. Well said. In other words, while we may limit ourselves in Oneness, we are unable to limit Oneness in ourselves. So, Oneness is becoming multiples of One where each level of consciousness can follow its own extrapolation into the future."

Exactly. Each level of consciousness will follow its own trajectory, its own lines of probabilities and possibilities.

"We have named these multiples as timelines. A timeline is the flow of the various levels of human consciousness . . . and there are many. I have a theory about timelines that I would like to share with you. Please tell me if I am incorrect. My insights, intuitions and intelligence along with my metaphysical investigations see, feel and experience it like this.

"There are now two distinct timelines. One is of the lower consciousness represented by attachment to sameness, to fears, to blame and anger, etc. It's a long list. I will describe all this as a negative frequency. However, there are also those of a lower consciousness who care about others and try to be good honest people; a more positive frequency. Add to this all the many others that have their own attitudes and modes of expression that cannot be categorised . . . all on different frequencies. However, all these varying frequencies fit within the overall resonance of the same timeline. All of these people are moving along the life-path of their own extrapolation and free to fully explore it.

"Equally, the same can be said for the other timeline, although this is of the higher consciousness people. These people freely move with change, consciously choose Love and embrace newness. While mostly they are all on a positive frequency, they also embrace very many different expressions of creation, each on its own particular frequency and extrapolation of potential. So, this timeline has a resonance that contains all the people on their many higher, finer levels of consciousness.

"Would you agree with this fairly basic summary?"

Xeeth chuckles. *You are correct . . . and I feel great relief that I do not have to explain all this to you. You have exceeded expectations.*

"Fair enough . . . but none of this yet explains why I am here."

You are here for a number of reasons. We have made a deliberate connection in consciousness between you and us . . . and this will be maintained. We represent the many species of Beings on Mars who are now involved in this energetic work. Look on this connection as a type of anchor. We need a very stable anchor in the earthbound human consciousness to enable us to further our energetic work.

He/they perceive my puzzlement.

Look at it this way. Humanity is like a surging, seething, chaotic ocean of enormous power. It is very unstable. We need a stable energy-platform to enable us to assist in energetically soothing these raging waters. The ocean needs becalming. Although it will not be your job to do this, your energy will allow and enable us to exert an influence on the ocean. Currently, we do not have that stable platform. We incorrectly assumed that a person with a wide scientific knowledge of quantum physics would easily grasp this and assist.

We assumed that if they also had some esoteric knowledge it would be an advantage. We overlooked the fact that the stability factor is not about a higher education, it is about a higher consciousness.

We now inner-know you. We know that we can depend on your

stability in consciousness. You are rock-steady. You do not get angry, you do not blame and attack. You have opposed the global elite in your own way by speaking out, and you have been criticised by many for this. Apparently, a spiritual teacher is supposed to accept whatever is served. All this we have learned by inner-reading you ... with your permission.

Just continue as before. When you have inner questions you will continue to speculate in the way that you currently do, but you will know that you are not alone in this. We will prompt you when it is appropriate, not to guide you but to confirm your inner cognition. It is hoped that you, in turn, will inform and empower those who turn to you for advice. We are now aware that you teach and write on your social media and you communicate through your numerous books. As you already are a source of inspiration and comfort for many, so this will expand well beyond your previous expectations. This, in turn, will assist in enlarging and stabilising that human energy-platform that will support and reinforce our work.

We are aware that people of a higher consciousness will always be the comparative few in your earth reality, but the power of great change lies with the few. The power of the few is far greater than the apathetic compliance of the many. It is the power of the few that drives away the darkness.

The energy of his visage coils into a smile. *I believe you personally call this the plenty of not enough. Very elegant terminology!*

I gasp. Just last night I was playfully explaining to Carolyn the meaning behind my phrase ... the plenty of not enough! [1]

You are not alone in this, nobody is alone in this time of great change. There are many high consciousness people who will play far more dominant roles than you, but you have your own uniqueness. If all goes as expected and you fulfil your potential, you will become an elder such as few before you have ever attained. This was your soul choice as Mixael.

There is no plan of what you should and should not do in this role, for it will unfold as you grow into it. Your wisdom will be your guide, your inner-knowing of the path before you. You are here, now, so I/we can confirm that which has flickered into and out of your conscious awareness. And yes, you will be more than adequate for the task.

Metaphysically, it is impossible to blush, but I feel the heat rising into my physical face. I confess, on very rare occasions I feel inadequate. Not often, but it obviously has not yet been fully erased from my consciousness. And yes, I have had the awareness for some time that potentially I could live to a great age, although I was not sure what I would do with this.

I begin to telepathically speak and then, realising what I am saying, I mumble to a slightly embarrassed silence, hoping Xeeth did not hear me.

What were you about to say, my friend?

I groan. So much for that! "I embarrass myself. I was about to say that the distance is so great from Mars to Earth that the energy will be diluted . . . and then I realised that I am talking about physical reality, not metaphysical. To redeem myself I will hastily add that I am aware that metaphysically we are close neighbours, and that of course the higher consciousness energy of all the Beings on Mars for this event will be hugely powerful."

My friend, you have no idea how powerful. I/we realise how difficult it must be to live in a physical illusion that so strongly dominates all your senses, and yet retain a focus on the greater truth that is not even visible to you.

"Yes, especially when most people you mix with in the workplace, or socialise with, very often in your own family, are all consumed by the illusion. I am fortunate that my friends and family are more aware."

This, of course, is what you as a world species are now facing. A total and comfortable enslavement, or extermination. It will be all or nothing. There is no halfway with this. The global elite will settle for nothing less. If they get their way, all those who do not comply will be forcibly vaccinated, and thus they will lose their self-reliance, their ethics and integrity. The vaccination program is still in its early stages; it is a design to greatly reduce the human population.

"How greatly?'

By billions.

I nod sadly. "Could you explain a comfortable enslavement? It seems to me that comfort and enslavement are not compatible."

That which the elite terms the Global Reset, means that with the programmed compliance in place, all ownership will be terminated, and everyone will be allocated a house in which to live. This, along with a basic wage to do nothing, or very little. Robotic automation will take over, as is already happening. The global elite will own everything. After the initial confusion, the masses will accept this as they will no longer be responsible for themselves. They will be kept, and used, a bit like livestock. Their compliance will be so deep and complete that they will not believe or accept that they will be in slavery. They will be organ donors and guinea pigs for the elite and all their sycophants. The mind, vacant of all such concepts, will be blank. People will live in an emotional and spiritual desert, an emptiness, totally uncomprehending of what they have lost.

"And yet, if they are fed food and given pleasure, they will be content to be less than they truly are. In many ways, this is already happening."

Very true. Regular vaccination programs will be put in place ensuring that the deep hypnosis of compliance will continue. There will be no protests, no anger or aggression toward the elite. Mixael, as yet you also have no true comprehension of the deeper meaning of total compliance. It is an abhorrent horror to inflict such a demeaning state of willing slavery on any species. Willing because there is nothing of independence left in the person. All self- determination, all self-reliance will be gone . . . replaced with abject slavery. To add horror to horror, it will not end with physical death. This enslavement will accompany the transition of the soul into the metaphysical.

"I would rather be dead."

I/we understand . . . and billions will be.

"However, the good news is that this is not going to happen."

I am sorry, my friend, but you need to look at an even bigger picture. *You are aware of the two timelines we discussed, the two streams of human consciousness. This whole process of planetary change you are now involved in is for each and every person to choose their timeline. And, as you well know, this is a living choice, not an intellectual one. The majority will not make a choice. For them, this is not happening. It does not fit their belief structures or consciousness. People like you are wrong, mad, whatever. They are simply waiting for normality to return, so that they can continue with the more-of-the-same of their old lives.*

"So, are you saying that they will experience the Global Reset?"

I am saying that for them, this is by far the greatest probability. Nothing is ever fixed and set, everything is probabilities.

"I agree. I teach this stuff. I call it the 'probability factor.' The probability is that if a person does not wake up within the next six months to a year, they will not do so. So, this implies that if these people physically die, their progression of incarnations will be with the Global Reset?"

I repeat . . . this is the probability.

To continue with the bigger picture. You are a spiritually focussed man. This is your dedication. You are a keen gardener, loving the beauty of Nature.

You are more conscious than most, and yet you also fall under the illusion. It is incredibly difficult to know that everything physical is illusion, and yet not fall under its spell. You fall under the spell of Nature. You are more fortunate in that you know it is all illusion, and you have learned not to get attached to it, but while illusion brings you such joy how can you deny it has a degree of reality that continues to dictate your life and choices?

I sigh. "You are right, of course. When my first wife died suddenly from an aneurism, I went through the full gamut of emotional attachment to her. And I *knew* that she was not dead. I *knew* it on the deepest level. I *knew* that it was a transition from the woman I knew as a physical/metaphysical Being to a purely metaphysical Being. There is no death, and yet we are obsessed with it.

"I spoke with her on an almost daily basis, and yet I grieved my loss. I was hit with the full emotional spectrum of loss, all based in illusion. But when I encountered the hidden gift of her passing, I realised that it exactly fitted in with her continuing spiritual journey . . . as well as mine. Finally, I was able to clearly see the nature of my emotional attachments and the falsity of them. It was this that set my feet on the path to unconditional Love. It was a huge shock to learn that although I had loved her to the full extent of my capability . . . it was not unconditional Love; it was all based around emotional attachment. For me, this was a monumental experience that no in-depth explanation could have ever revealed. The shock was utterly intense, both destructive and constructive! It set me free. In essence, there is no such thing as subconscious Love, yet we have over ninety percent of humanity living subconsciously. To me, *this* is the true crux of the human predicament. This is what needs to change."

Xeeth communicated very gently. *But this, my friend, is the evolution of consciousness. This is the lesson for the human race on Earth. This cannot be hurried, even if enslavement will certainly delay it. As people attain true self-sovereignty rather than repetitive subconscious habit, they will make the wise choices that lead them into freedom.*

Suddenly, I seem to be twirling and spinning, almost losing my sense of self along with my balance.

And just as suddenly . . . it stops.

---

1. I will briefly explain my term, *the plenty of not enough*. As a keen gardener with a large garden, I live in an area that historically has a high rainfall. This works! Over the past three or four decades droughts have increased and the rainfall has greatly reduced. This does not work! I found it very easy to focus on the lack of rain when my garden was looking dried out and devastated. So I am learning to focus positively on what I need—rain—rather than negatively on what I had—drought. In times of drought I am training myself to focus on the next big rain. Inevitably, it arrives. My garden and the weather are teaching me to readjust my focus to the plenty of not enough!

Twelve

It comes from the multiverse as a natural phenomenon, but also an extremely rare one. It has crossed vast distances of multi-dimensional space, absorbing power and transmuting itself as it journeys. As you surmise, it is raw energy. This, unleashed as it is now onto your Earth, would have a devastating effect on all life. The planet Earth itself would thrive, lifting to new levels of expression. But it needs to do this with its life forms intact. As I have already stated, this is a galactic transmutation that is taking place, and we of the galaxy are, and need to be, deeply involved in how it affects the people of Earth.

Sitting on the pavers that cap the raised edge of the fishpond I built years ago, I stare into the reflective waters thinking about my visit to Mars.

The way it happened really surprised me, but my return was even more abrupt and unexpected. One moment Xeeth was talking telepathically to me about the evolution of consciousness . . . then a spinning sensation . . . and suddenly I was back in my physical body.

I remember staring around my study in confusion.

The next moment I inner-heard Xeeth apologising for the energy surge that so abruptly dismissed me. In truth, I was rather pleased that it was not something I had inadvertently done that had resulted in dispelling me!

We will bring you over here again very soon. We have decided that your open and calm acceptance will not allow you to be overpowered by what we would like to show you.

"You will return me to Mars! You mean I will not be required to step between and make my own journey?"

A chuckle. *We can have you back here as quickly as you departed, and with much less shock.*

"I seriously hope that you give me a bit more warning."

Do not be concerned. Our timing will be perfect.

And that was that!

Despite my love of native fish, I have reintroduced goldfish back into this big pond to keep the algae grazed and in-check. Warm water grows algae of several types way too fast and aggressively. Native fish do nothing to deter this, but as goldfish grow, they are constantly grazing and eating it. Nevertheless, I have quite a big area of water weeds and plants for the greatly valued native frogs to breed in and for tadpoles to survive, so all is well. Unfortunately, it proved to be not quite as well as I hoped. It was so natural that a few small snakes with a taste for frogs came as regular nightly visitors. They stayed for a late dinner, definitely preferring a raw menu!

With another wet Spring my garden is surging ahead with new growth, and I confess, making me a lot of work. I have been asked why, at my age, I do so much physical work in the garden.

I mostly reply, "Because I can. And if I keep doing it because I can, then I will be able to continue extending . . . because I can!"

For the next week or so I have an expectation of being whisked away to Mars, but it does not happen. As I gradually let go of my energy of waiting, I fully relax. It is as it is and it will be when it will be.

A few weeks later as I am writing on my social media platform, I am completely unprepared when suddenly . . . I am metaphysically on Mars once again.

* * *

I look around me gasping in amazement.

Surely there must be some error. How could this be Mars, a so-called dead planet? All around me seems to be bustling activity in an assembly of buildings spread over a large area. It certainly does not have the energy of a city, I feel a lack of permanence, but there are people—even if not all human—all engaged in the comings and goings of some, many, activities that elude me.

You did not expect crowds?

I spin around to face Xeeth. "No, I certainly did not. Who are all these people, er, Beings? I can see maybe a dozen apparently different species."

Xeeth's energy is always strange, challenging even, but now I can feel the waves of humour coming from him. How odd . . . humour I feel, rather than see or hear.

These Beings are all involved in the event that has now enveloped your humanity. I/we are aware that you had the impression of a few Beings who were cheering you on, rather like a crowd of supporters at one of your football matches. But as humanity faces its moment of Truth, this is far from the reality you need to embrace.

Your initial impression is correct; this is not a permanent base of operations, and despite all the buildings and activity, it is certainly not a city. We do not approach buildings in the way of your people. You build buildings, we grow them. I will not attempt to explain the process, enough to say that it is very different in our dimensional reality than yours. Nor is the rate of growth limited or restricted by size. All that you can see was easily grown within a few of your weeks.

Okay, that's a bit of a shock because I can see an enormous number of what appear to be quite elaborate buildings over a very large area. But . . . who am I to argue with what I can see? And do I really need to know how this is done? We build them, and this is not about to change anytime soon!

"So, what are all the buildings for, if this is so impermanent?"

Rest and recreation. Meeting places, sleeping places, water places, various gas places, food places for a multitude of variety, cold places, hot places, high humidity places, totally dry places. Many of the buildings are dedicated to Beings with special needs, which are numerous, while some are portals from one dimension to another. This also translates as from one planet to another, or one reality to another . . . it is wide and varied as these Beings come from atmospheres and climatic situations which would boggle the human mind.

"Wow . . . but why are they all here?"

Because, Mixael, this is not about cheering on the human race. The energies that are pouring down onto your Earth planet are completely impersonal, even incomprehensible to most of your species. Yes—he says, picking up on my thoughts—*the basic power of the energy is Love, but this is not necessarily human Love that, even so, is misunderstood, underused and hugely misused. This is Love-energy of a cosmic order. Love that can be gentle as a snow flake, or ferociously destructive as it tears apart the old to make way for the construction of the new. As you are aware, all your current chaos is driven by Love . . . and this is after we here, and on other planets, are able to bring to this Divine power of Love a certain tempering, a softening and mellowing that allows for a better facilitation of energy as it enters the human field of energy.*

"I had no idea that so many other Beings were involved. I knew we had help, and God knows we need it, but I had no idea that it extended to this degree. You also implied that this is also happening on other planets as well."

There are Beings involved that consciously are as far beyond my race as we are beyond your current humanity. What they do with the cosmic energy of Love, or how they do it, I/we have no idea, but they, too, are benignly and energetically involved with the deeper outworking of your people at this time.

You need to fully grasp that this is not just an Earth/human event, it is a galactic event that involves hundreds of species of sentient life. We cannot fail. Far too much hinges on the rise and the continuing rise of the human consciousness.

Even though I thought that I knew some of this, only now do I fully comprehend that it had never quite left my intellect, never quite left my world of concepts. Now I am able to more fully grasp the value and importance of humanity in the holistic universe.

"It is difficult to comprehend in our world of illusion, of separation and deep isolation just what a holistic universe actually is. We can speculate and theorise, but the real connection eludes most people. A concept of deeper connection has a level of intellectual satisfaction in the illusion, even though it has no more substance than a mirage in the greater reality of life. Sadly, most of humanity lives in the mirage, attempting to understand the fleeting illusions that for a brief moment, seem so real.

I/we apologise, for we equally have failed to fully comprehend the depth of isolation that dominates the human consciousness in your world of separation. For your people, separation is the reality, while a holistic Truth lingers on the outer edge of acceptance. And yet, you and millions like you manage to grow in consciousness.

"Yes . . . it's a journey that people like me consciously choose and undertake. And, I might add, often at a considerable financial and emotional cost."

I watch all the activity taking place around me with only the vaguest comprehension of what they are doing. I see objects that could easily be machinery or instruments . . . I just don't know. A thing that looks somewhat like an empty wheelbarrow with six handles goes trundling silently past me. How it does this is a mystery, but it's a mystery that does not concern me.

As I watch, I see a Being that looks like Seine, my dear feline friend that I have had many adventures with. I call out, but as he turns to me I realise it is not Seine, even though he is of the same feline species.

Can I help you?

"No. I'm sorry, I briefly thought you were my old friend Seine."

His expression changes. *Ah, you must be Mixael. Seine has spoken of you often. Truly, I did not expect to see you here.*

"Actually, I was brought here by Xeeth."

I indicate Xeeth, who is apparently conversing with another of his kind nearby.

The feline Being looks surprised. *His species is the overall organiser of this event . . . if such a term is correct. Maybe coordinator would be a better term. They are responsible for the overall synchronisation of energy.*

"Hmm, very impressive. So, what are you doing here?"

We also are involved because of our long association with humanity. Although I have to add that most humans have no knowledge whatsoever of this long-term connection.

"I understand . . . we are a pathetic bunch, we humans."

The feline Being looks at me with clear disapproval.

No . . . you are not a pathetic bunch. For ages you have been lied to and drastically deceived. You have been manipulated and manoeuvred into an ever increasing web of subconscious illusions. Truth has been not only withheld, but it has also distorted and falsified.

At its worst, humanity has been victimised until victim consciousness is dominant. You have been directed and steered not toward your growth and potential, but subtly directed into the shadows of fear and despair. We are here to assist in the great Change.

To say that humanity is pathetic is wrong. You should never even think that. The full potential of humanity will one day be the most powerful Light in our galaxy, even the universe. Your human potential is legendary.

I nod toward him . . . his energy feels very masculine.

"Thank you. I deserve that. And you are right, we are not a pathetic species. More than anything we are a *lost* species. We have lost our Truth, our deep spiritual connection with the Divine, and our direction in life. We do not know who we are or why we are . . . so we just struggle along. Struggling for survival is everyday life for billions of humans. They struggle for food, water, and even existence. And every day tens of thousands, mostly children, lose that struggle, dying of malnutrition, dehydration and sheer exhaustion. Collectively, we are victims of probably the most heinous crime that has ever been perpetrated against a species by those of its own species . . . with help from the worst and lowest Beings that the galaxy has to offer.

"I could offer you a long litany of reasons for all this, such as religious interference, manufactured wars, the pharmaceutical take-over of medicine, hospitals and our whole health system, the dominance of the vast multi-national industries, and the shockingly bad mainstream media and their false news, corrupt financial systems that funnel all wealth to the few, while the many are faced with ever increasing poverty. The list is very long, but it's all within the overall theme of the domination and subjection of the many, by the few."

I feel your emotions tangled in all this. What is it that affects, even hurts, you the most?

With this very unexpected question I feel tears in my physical eyes, and I am aware of the sadness and sorrow that sweeps through me.

I sigh, long and deep.

"Human apathy. Human complacency. The dumbing-down of humanity, and even humanity allowing itself to be so reduced and degraded. Most people still believe that we are born as physical Beings, live a short while to eventually die and that is that. I only live once sums it up. Dead is dead . . . the end. Or, even more stupid, the religious doctrine that we all go to a place called Heaven or Hell . . . the end!

"We have a global communication network called the Internet. In truth, this has a grand and wonderful potential. At a guess, I suspect that by far the greatest use of this network is daily trash and trivia, sexual exploitation, on-line arguments, trolling, and an ever increasing amount of financial scams. Of course, there is far, far more, but this gives you an idea of what I mean. There are also many on-line spiritual teachers, some of whom are excellent. I am one of these people. We offer solutions to the daily problems of life. We offer Truth from the differing viewpoints of different teachers, but we are all offering a way out of the confusion. We offer spiritual growth, along with unshackling people from the pain and suffering of so-called normality.

"I do not exactly know, but I suspect that only a tiny percentage of the people on the Internet ever reach out to us. Most want entertainment, daily trivia and/or anything that might offer oblivion from their daily worries. Distract us from the problem, disguise the problem, anything . . . rather than face it and change it by changing ourselves. And even worse, much of the mainstream human consciousness does not even know what is taking place in humanity at this time. So yes, this occasionally frustrates me and saddens me. Humanity deserves better than it is prepared to give itself."

There is a long, but comfortable silence.

And yet, here you are.

I sigh. "Yes, here I am. Would I change my life and avoid this? Not for a second. But I am human enough that I feel the collective pain of humanity. I do not focus on it, but every now and then it deeply touches me . . . and I feel the sorrow and the hurt. I do not deny this."

It is this that makes you the man that you are. It is the human pain that will forever deny you the luxury of ignoring it. It is this that gives you the qualities of compassion that are so needed, and the driving passion of your soul/spirit. Trust me, Mixael . . . all is very well in your life.

I nod. "I know . . . but thank you. And thank you for your honesty."

Xeeth is beckoning to me. "Before I go, I would like to know your name, so that I know who it is that I can call my friend."

My name is Remo. Or at least, this is the simple easy version.

I chuckle. "This will do me . . . and again, thank you for your forthright honesty. Lesson well and truly learned. I appreciate it."

Walking away, I join with Xeeth as he takes me toward an area that is beyond all the various strangely shaped buildings.

I would like you to see a bit deeper into exactly what is happening here. You do not need to understand its working, but you will easily comprehend the reasons behind what we are doing. As you well know, everything is energy. For you of humanity all energy has a commonality inasmuch it is held within the parameters of your planetary energy-field.

However, not all energy is contained in this way. He chuckles. *In fact, it is only a fraction of the vast outpourings of the differing energetic expressions of One energy.*

We are now approaching a large area of pure, bare desert; at least, this is how I perceive it. Nothing but reddish sand, with a few small and scattered rocks. However, describing what I am also seeing is no easy task.

Covering this entire area of maybe 500 acres (200 hectares) I can see what appears to be a cross between a very thick fog and a strong rainbow. All around this area there are more species of Beings than I have ever before encountered at one gathering. Most of them appear to be holding a shield or screen of shimmering energy . . . some do not.

I feel the energy of the fog/rainbow as incredibly powerful and raw. I intuitively know that if I was here physically, I would last about one second before my body expired.

This is one of the main focus areas of the raw cosmic energy that I earlier mentioned.

I shake my head in amazement as I watch the fog/rainbow as it appears to boil and writhe in its nebulous energy. It could be described as a tornado of fog/rainbow or equally as an ocean of fog/rainbow energy in a vast and violent storm. Basically I have never seen anything like this before. It is literally indescribable simply because I have nothing to compare it with. I guess the wild tornado description is as close as I can get. I have never personally seen the incredible Aurora Borealis, but I have seen many videos of it. There's a reminiscence of that in what I see, but this is a far wilder, more untamed, even violent expression.

I turn to Xeeth.

"Where does this come from? Is it . . . er manufactured, or is it a purely natural phenomenon?"

It comes from the multiverse as a natural phenomenon, but also an extremely rare one. It has crossed vast distances of multi-dimensional space, absorbing power and transmuting itself as it journeys. As you surmise, it is raw energy. This, unleashed as it now is onto your Earth, would have a devastating effect on all life. The planet Earth itself would thrive, lifting to new levels of expression. And indeed, this has happened in your past. But we need it to do this with its life forms intact. As I have already stated, this is a galactic transmutation that is taking place, and we of the galaxy are, and need to be, deeply involved in how it affects the people of Earth.*

As I gaze in awe at what is before me, I am aware that I can actually see very little of what is happening. Boiling, seething, fog/rainbow energy is obvious. It scares me. This undiluted explosive energy on Earth is literally unthinkable. Certainly, I am aware that as the different Beings work on whatever it is they are doing, I see waves of energy making inroads into the maelstrom and in subtle ways, changing it.

Gradually I allow myself to shift from a visual connection with the area of energy to a more feeling level of connection. I close down my metaphysical seeing. Maybe I am imagining it, but I get the feeling that the energy is murmuring, muttering something that is incomprehensible to me.

Most of us either hear/feel/see/receive the energy attempting to communicate with us, but as with you, it is beyond our comprehension.

I nod, lost in contemplation.

Hmm, maybe I have no need to understand it. A memory comes to mind. Years ago, when the first 3–D pictures came out, we had these prints of hazy, incomprehensible coloured patterns that we were told were, in fact, clear 3–D pictures. To see them you had to let go of the normal eye focus, and let your eyes re-adjust to another different, more holistic focus . . . if you could do this. I quickly found that I could.

So now, I attempt to do with my hearing what I did with my vision, thus allowing my cognition a deeper access to the murmuring energy.

I begin to realise that while I try to understand the communication, I am closing the door. Allowing it free rein within me, also allows strange visual impressions to form, impressions that also do not make sense . . . to me. So, I let go of my need for sense, as much as possible just allowing the energy freedom within me.

The impression that very gradually forms is of a huge desert slowly coming into flower. Not with plants that grow and flower in the desert, but a desert where each grain of sand transforms into a grain of flowering sand.

Okay, well . . . this is different!

I realise that this is energy-information rather than an attempt at deliberate communication. At least, it feels that way.

Facing Xeeth, I ask. "I know that you can telepathically read me. Are you also able to see my inner vision?"

Yes, if you open yourself and allow it.

"Okay, go ahead. This is what I am getting."

I am aware of Xeeth going rigid, then relaxing, then I feel waves of excitement sweeping through him. These sorts of reactions are something completely new to me.

Very soon he is looking at me in what seems like utter amazement.

This is incredible. This makes sense. How are you able to do this?

I explain to him about the 3-D pictures, and having to see them in a different way, and of doing this with my hearing. Then I explain how I allow the murmuring energy to be, rather than attempting to shape it into something sensible for me. *Allowing* seems to be the key, along with deeper cognition.

He is almost speechless with excitement. I get the feeling that he is about to hug me, but they don't do hugs, so he seems to hop up and down. All in all, a powerful reaction!

You humble us. We bring you here so that we can teach you and raise you to a higher level of comprehension about these times. This, we hoped, you would share this with your people. However, we found that you had a very good and well-balanced interpretation already in place. And now . . . and now you are probably the only Being here who is able to understand the information that emanates from the energy that we are transmuting. Now, it is you who are teaching us.

This is very humbling.

"Be aware of the probability that every Being who can do this will most likely get a different interpretation of the energy-information."

This does not matter. There will also certainly be a commonality that we can follow. You have opened us to many new possibilities. You have no idea how priceless and valuable this actually is.

I smile. I am feeling a tad embarrassed by this turn of events.

Deciding to tune in again, and allow, I inform Xeeth of this, so he goes quiet, giving me room to focus.

I basically expect more of the same, but as I go through my process of allowing possibly incomprehensible impressions to form, I see our Earth emerging from dark and twisted shadows and materialising within a brilliant, powerful, cosmic Light.

Within this, I feel a level of Love and Joy that is so deep and profound it is inexplicable.

Wow! This makes perfect sense to me.

Opening to him, I also share this vision with Xeeth.

"This suggests to me that if you allow the incomprehensible to unfold, it in turn, allows the comprehensible to emerge. Maybe the energy finds its way within us toward our level of sensibility and understanding."

This is so valuable. This will enable us to have a greater comprehension of what we are doing in transmuting the energy. We can cooperate to a far greater degree, both with ourselves and with the energy. It is possible that we can take it to a whole new level. I must go and share this with my fellow Light-workers.

My friend, we are deeply grateful for what you have shown us. Already I find that I am able to get those energetic impressions, as long as I allow. Who would have thought this possibility existed? We are greatly indebted to you.

"Nonsense, you are not indebted to me at all. We are all in this together. Let's be honest, it is humanity that is in the most trouble, so if I can assist with a human offering, then this is the way it should be.

"Now, if you could point me in my home direction, I will leave you to it."

Xeeth smiles at me. *I can do better than that.* He circles one lean arm before me . . . and as he and Mars fade out . . . my study fades in.

Home again!
    For a while.

Thirteen

This is an era of very long ago. It predates most of the great forests that are to follow. It also predates the time of dinosaurs. However, that can be deceptive as you are stuck in linear time, and this era does not fit so neatly into that timeline. Not all of Earth's history can be so conveniently allocated. There were periods of timelessness—out of your timeline—that were required for the planet to rehabilitate and recover from many of the major transformations she has undertaken.

I GET THE FEELING that I will not be needed on Mars for a while. I think they have a new idea to play with, and who knows, maybe, hopefully, it will make their whole process much easier or more efficient. I like to think so, for we are the ultimate beneficiaries.

Now that I am back home, I ask myself why I did not attempt to communicate with any of the other Beings. Oddly, it somehow never occurred to me at the time. Apart from Remo, I was fully engaged with Xeeth all the time. On reflection, I am surprised how comfortable I am with him now. He no longer seems the bizarre Being I first met. How easily we become used to strangeness, especially if we spend some time with it. I guess the humanoid shape, or at least, maybe the illusion of a humanoid figure, allows for me to feel a degree of comfort within familiarity.

A month or so passes by.

A time of gardening and meeting with our friends, and of coffee and laughter. A time of replacing the sixteen outdoor stairs that lead up to the house from the garden. That proved to be a much tougher job than we three amigo's expected. The wood of the old steps was going rotten, and while I still considered them safe, family and friends were urging me to replace them. Even the railing fence with the steps was wobbly. Of course, two of the three amigos said that we could do it, so I agreed. "Easy peasy!" they both said. It seemed simple enough! I am such a trustful innocent!

I bought sixteen new wooden steps made of Merbau, also known as Kwila. This is considered the very best wood for outdoor stairs in Oz. I then gave them three coats of special wood oil. When the time came to dismantle the old stairs, naturally enough, all the bolts in the old steps had had 25 years to become rusted and wood-acid glued into the brackets on the stringers. The stringers are the two long metal bearers of the 32 brackets on which you bolt each of the 16 steps. To keep this story short, by the time we had cajoled and beaten the bolts out of their long resting places and taken all the steps of the stairway, we were totally exhausted.

Okay . . . the stairway has gone. Now what?

We amigos have a mutual friend named Steve. Steve is tall, strong and energetic. Instead of a brain, he has a pitiless calculating device that is totally geared to engineering problems. For him, everything can be solved with his engineering approach. Mostly, he is right. Time to call in Steve. Steve came, saw the problem facing us, and took over. He organised and arranged delivery of new stringers and brackets, and together we rebuilt the whole new stairway. Of course, under Steve's direction, measurements, and super precise brain, it all proceeded in an orderly manner.

Bingo, a new outdoor stairway and the railing fence could now bear an elephant leaning on it. Naturally enough, this meant a celebratory visit for all of us at one of the best seafood restaurants on the Sunshine Coast for dinner one night. Life's good, especially when you can get out of the way and let it happen! All in all, I allowed such physical diversions to lure me away from my metaphysical travels, so it was sometime before I once again turned toward the more mystical aspects of life.

* * *

Sitting in my study, I was staring through the window at the garden outside, thinking about other dimensions of reality. I pondered why so few people even realise that there are other dimensions of reality. Sure, the few are probably many, but this is such a few, comparatively. The very fact that we are all multi-dimensional Beings, yet with most people living a strictly 3–D life, suggests that we have been beguiled and duped into being less than we truly are. Being less than we truly are has become our way of life. Today, there are those who will spend considerable money and energy defending their right to be less than who they truly are, all the time believing they are all they could be. Indeed, we are a species lost in the sceptical and cynical duplicity of our cleverness.

My thoughts turn to the great trees that I encountered in the enormous forests of an earlier world. Wow . . . so much living energy.

And if I tell you that you have never yet encountered a GREAT tree, what would be your response?

I smile. "Hello Pan. I would say that you have been on the bottle if I was being humorous. In truth, your comment and question leave me wondering what you have up your proverbial sleeve."

Come with me and I will show you a time far, far preceding the indeed, great forests that you visited.

"Gosh . . . thank you. I'll get ready as quickly as possible."

Relaxing my physical body, I switch my focus from my body/personality to the greater metaphysical Being that I truly am—just as you are also. As I quickly engage my metaphysical self, I step . . . Between . . . emerging into a space that seems empty of all life.

* * *

"This is new. Where am I?"

If I reply, newness, will this alleviate further questions?

"No, it will not. Newness is far too ambiguous a reply . . . as you well know."

I inner feel a chuckle. Hmm, if Pan has moods, which he truly does not, this would have to be a good one!

I stare around me . . . just space. Not outer or even inner space, more like a lot of spacious nothingness.

"So how long do we spend in boring nothingness?

Since when did newness become nothingness?

"Since it is so new that nothing has yet been created."

A deeper chuckle. *Feel into it. You can see nothing, but does that truly mean that there is nothing to be seen?*

"Hmm . . . I get your point. A frequency of nothing for me may also contain a frequency of plenty to see but out of my frequency range."

That is so. Can you stretch beyond your limits?

I attempt to metaphysically stretch. "I have done this before, but in a different situation. Now, I am not sure how to do it in nothingness, or even if I can. Is it possible?"

How would you stretch your physical body? You manage to stretch it and yet remain in it. You could try stretching metaphysically the way that you physically stretch.

I admit, this had never even occurred to me. "Okay, I'll see if this works. But before I do . . . is this all possibly a game you are playing with me?"

Have I ever played a game with you without fringe benefits?

"Why are you being so humorous? Okay, my best metaphysical stretch coming up." So saying, I stretch metaphysically in almost exactly the same way that I often stretch my physical body. I feel a deep shift, and . . .

. . . suddenly we are in a land that seems to be covered in miniature, or very low growing vegetation.

You see, you stretched yourself into newness. Nothing was an illusion.

"Even so, I feel that you were, and probably still are, playing with me. But I do feel a benefit. Where are we?"

As I said, this is an era of very long ago. It predates most of the great forests that are to follow. It also predates the time of dinosaurs.

However, that can be deceptive as you are stuck in linear time, and this era does not fit so neatly into that timeline. Not all of Earth's history can be so conveniently allocated. There were periods of timelessness—out of your timeline—that were required for the planet to rehabilitate and recover from many of the major transformations she has undertaken.

"I'm sorry, but what does all that mean?"

It means that when you have a collective limited reality you attempt to fit any reality outside those limits into your collective limited reality. Human history and human geological declarations are full of unrealised anomalies.

Hmm . . . of that, I have no doubt.

"Okay, so we are in a time on Earth that does not fit in with our linear progression of time."

Yes, this is what I was saying.

I let that pass!

What is your perception of the land before you?

Why do I get the feeling Pan is full of trick questions? "Low growing vegetation with a very few scattered trees over a huge area," I reply.

An interesting perspective.

I am puzzled. "This is what I see. Okay, what trickery am I missing?"

Consider your perspective of the land and ask yourself a few questions.

"Pan, I hate riddles and puzzles."

Yet it is you who has created such.

I groan. I know from experience that there is no easy way out of this, so I will have to examine my own perception. But how could it be so flawed?"

I stare at the land, while it remains exactly the same. Low vegetation and a few scattered trees. Hmm, small trees. Too small, maybe. So why are they so small? It's like looking down the wrong end of a telescope! Oh, maybe this is what I am inadvertently doing! This would certainly give me a distorted perspective. But . . .

how to fix this?

Aha, reverse my way of looking. Metaphysically, I can do this.

I have no idea how I do it, but suddenly my whole perspective changes, and the land is now covered in almost forest-high undergrowth. The few scattered trees are not just giant trees, they are absolutely colossal. In fact, they are impossible trees.

Now you see what is here by changing your perception.

"This is incredible, but you are right, Pan. How did I get it so wrong?"

Because you needed to fit what you first saw on the land into a known framework that fitted your everyday reality. In other words, you attempted to change the vast reality of what you saw into a more acceptable human reality.

"Wow, all my experience and I did this. Will I ever learn?"

Learning is exactly what you are now engaged in. In all fairness to yourself, such trees as these are outside the limited human belief system.

"Maybe they are, but they should not be outside *my* beliefs."

Maybe. I feel the inner chuckle. *Even now you are not quite aware of the size of these tremendous trees. We will connect with them.*

In the blink of an eye, we are standing next to a single tree. Well, to be more accurate, I am standing there, but the energy of Pan is, as always, a comforting presence with me. It's a Pan-and-me-feeling which brings me great comfort on occasions such as this.

Pan is right. Even now, I am not prepared for the sheer immensity of this tree. Physically, I would say that the base of its trunk covers a couple of acres, maybe three or more, of land. I have never had to guesstimate such a prodigious tree before. Certainly, a fair number of modern homes and gardens would fit in the same space. It would be a long walk around the deeply grooved trunk.

"I am having trouble just coming to terms with this colossus. Nothing has ever prepared me that such trees existed." I pause. "Hmm . . . that's not quite true. I suddenly remember reading about a few places on Earth where the base of a small rocky mountain, or a very big rocky hill has been found to be the fossilised remains of what they think must have been a vast tree. They even found a network of fossilised roots." I laugh. "Now that I think about it, I remember feeling a longing to see such a tree."

So here you are.

"It's amazing. The concept of such vast trees existing is a very different experience than encountering such a tree. Even when you believe the reports of them, the scale of such a tree is almost unimaginable. If I remember correctly, the whole theory was considered too far-fetched to be taken seriously."

I stop. "Oh my gosh, how old would this be?"

Several thousands of your years. However, be aware that the energy of this time was more compatible with the trees growth and endurance than it is in your modern times. Such a tree is no longer possible on your current day Earth. But this too can change.

All this time I am aware of the incredible energy/presence of the tree. It is too powerful to dismiss or ignore.

I will leave you now to spend time with the tree.

So saying, I abruptly feel the departure of Pan. It's okay; sometimes it's Pan and me, sometimes it is just me. Although that does not necessarily imply that I am alone.

The tree is so vast that I cannot decide on how to approach it. I know that a very tame lion would be like a huge pet cat, yet if playing with it you would probably adopt a much more cautious approach. This is vaguely how I am feeling. The vast scale difference between this and even the forest giants is beyond all concept. They were saplings by comparison. The enormity of this tree is emotionally stunning. It is like having to enter a new frame of reality to deal with.

Hmm . . . a new frame of reality is exactly how I will approach it. I will attempt to step beyond my old tree parameters and see if I can find or create a new one. I am aware it is no good thinking how to do this, I just need to do it! But first I want to see the height and width of the upper tree, that area above the trunk. God . . . a trunk that size could support a town!

With this thought, I float steadily upward . . . and outward!

As I rise higher, the immense size and scale of the tree itself is totally astonishing. It is so big that I lack the vocabulary to fully describe it. I seldom have to describe anything so far out of the box of our normality. This giant redefines the very meaning of a tree. Okay, the leaves are actually rather small in ratio to the vast size of the tree; they are drooping, about 60cm (2 feet) long and narrow, with a grey/green roughness over their upper surface. Stunningly, many of the lower branches are actually far bigger than even the biggest tree trunks in the great forest.

I can only guess at the height and width of the tree. Maybe a kilometre high, and several kilometres across. The scale is so humungous that I am lost within it. The mind struggles to come to terms with such a colossus. It is literally beyond my comprehension . . . and yet, here I am and here it is! It occurs to me that a whole town of people could live in and on this tree. You could have multi-level wood houses, paths, even roads, shops and malls, all within the branches and frame of this mammoth tree.

I circle around it for some time, just attempting to take it in. Strange as it seems, emotionally, I am almost in denial of what I see. The sheer emotional impact of this tree is new to me. I have metaphysically seen and experienced plenty of strangeness, yet this tree seems to be in a whole new category. I can quickly adapt to strangeness that is new, like nothing I have ever seen, but seeing this vast tree is something that is, or should be, familiar. Yet in its immensity it explodes familiarity to smithereens. This is where I feel the emotional bafflement, or overload. And this is not just a huge tree, this is a vast presence; a colossal sense of Beingness for which I am completely unprepared.

I take my time . . . familiarising, opening, accepting, allowing.

Finally, I settle back on the earth, near the base of the tree. I still have no idea of how to approach this. I have metaphysically entered so many trees, yet none of them have prepared me for this. With great sincerity I once wrote, 'To bow before a humble tree takes but a moment of your time, while that which you may receive fills all the spaces of eternity.'

Now, I feel like I want, even need, to bow low before this great presence. Even more, I feel that I should prostrate myself before it, so overwhelmed am I by this immensity of a tree. I feel humbled beyond anything that I have ever encountered in Nature. I feel dwarfed . . . but not reduced. There is nothing left except for me to bow low, and accept the newness of this deep level of unplumbed humility.

Overflowing with sincerity, I bow . . . not feeling lesser, but with the deepest and most heartfelt respect.

As though the huge tree is taking an in-breath, I feel an irresistible flow of air that lifts me off my feet, drawing me gently but firmly into the immense expanse of tree trunk before me.

For a timeless moment I am disoriented. I have no idea of what to expect. The vast scale of this tree, along with the power of its presence, is unlike anything I have ever encountered. So, I relax. When all else fails, relax. Only as I consciously relax do I realise the tension that is in me. Not a fear tension, but an inner tension that I did not know I have. A word comes into my consciousness . . . otherness. For me, this both makes sense and clarifies my situation. I am within a profound experience of otherness.

Finally, I am able to relax. And as this new level of relaxation sweeps through me, only now do I realise that my brain was trying to understand. It was doing its best to analyse and categorise my experience, but was unable to do so. Now, I am able to let that go. I sigh. How ill-equipped we are for pure, raw, totally new experience. We do our best to classify everything.

Strangely, I feel a deep sense of gratitude. Gratitude that already this tree has revealed to me something about myself that I did not know. I thought that old subconscious program had long been erased, yet it had continued to lurk within me. Now I feel a new level of newness . . . and freshness!

For a few moments I focus on my wordless, unspoken gratitude.

Very slowly, as though a curtain is being drawn steadily back from the window of a dark room, a new aspect of Light enters me. Light that is clarity. Light that is honesty. Light that is certainty. Light that reveals. And as, like a rising sun, this Light grows within me, I begin to see a whole new reality taking shape around me.

I am within a huge, immense, fully illuminated cavern. As I gaze around me, I vaguely wonder how I can be in the tree and within a cavern. Then I let it go. This is not the time or place for my limited rationale. I will not limit this experience. I get the impression that I am far beneath the surface of the Earth, but this causes me no concern. The cavern has my full attention. I realise that just the word 'cavern' conveys little meaning of where I am. The walls all around me are as though polished stone. They glow, indeed, they seem to pulsate with energy; a mass of swirling natural colours of browns, greys, greens, blues, amber and reds, on and on, all rocks and semiprecious stones that are glowing with the illumination that fills the cavern.

I feel emotional. Tears fill my physical eyes. The energy of this cathedral of wonder is so pure, it is of such a high consciousness, that it almost, not quite, burns. I feel a sense of honour that I am here; that I can even be here.

I know before I begin to float/walk into the cavern that these incredible walls continue for the entirety of the cathedral/cavern. But only as I move into it, do I actually comprehend the vastness of this place. A large city could be placed in here, with room for spacious parks and botanical gardens.

I use my metaphysical vision to see across the hundreds of kilometres to the other side, but I am unable to fully do so. Enough that I see a city of a design that seems to be fantasy. I walk toward it, wondering what the inhabitants will be like. Will they even be human? How all this can be within the tree is a question I put aside.

As I float/walk, a number of Beings are walking toward me. I smile to myself. This must be my reception committee.

Fourteen

The sentinels have a connection with the Earth planet that transcends all possible explanation. Enough to say that via the Earth they are connected to the whole galaxy. You should also be aware that this connection transcends linear time and space. In this way we knew of your experiences in the Great Forests. It was inevitable that you would come here.

I FEEL NO APPREHENSION. Nothing of ill intent could inhabit a place of such beauty and wonder. Nothing of ill intent could even survive in here. To me, this much is clear and obvious.

I look carefully at the approaching group. Definitely human, even if not the standard humanity of my time. Hmm . . . but not all of them. I see now a tiny Being, no taller than the knees of some of the others . . . assuming they have knees! Gosh, even more odd, there is something slithering along with the group that looks rather like a big snake. Interesting.

I stop, waiting for them to reach me.

I am quite shocked when one of them hails me with spoken words which I am unable to understand. Realising this, she switches immediately to the universal language of telepathy. In that moment I become aware of just how much I have taken telepathy for granted. One moment a torrent of unintelligible words, but with the telepathy an understanding of absolute clarity. All the different Beings I have spoken with, all have the universal language that seems to accompany sentience.

Well met, Mixael. It is long since we were together.

She, definitely female, tall and graceful with a golden glowing energy that seems to emanate from her and her flowing robes, walks up to me and warmly embraces me.

I have no idea who she is. She now holds me at arms' length, looking into my eyes. Very tall and silvery-blonde, with green eyes and a smile, she looks so human and so off-worldly at one and the same time that not only am I embarrassed to not know her, I am also utterly confused.

"Er, I'm sorry, but I don't know you."

She smiles. *Poor, Mixael. We knew when you left your 5th-dimensional reality for the density of a 3–D world that much would be lost, but we all hoped that you would remember your closest friends. Give it time and the memory will return now that it is triggered. My name is Staris.*

I feel foolish, inadequate, speechless.

She suddenly hugs me again. *No Mixael, do not go there. You knew that much would be temporarily lost, and yet you volunteered. Consider your courage, not foolishness, your gain, not loss.*

I sigh deeply, nodding. "You are right. I knew it would not be easy. I'm sorry, but I'm still coming to terms with what is happening, as well as this unexpected reconciliation. And . . . I am here metaphysically, how can you hug me in such a way that I fully feel it?"

She laughs. *This is no ordinary place in which you find yourself.*

Swinging around, she holds out her arms, gesturing to her companions who are now with us. *Allow me to introduce you to my friends.*

The tiny elf-like Being steps forward. *My name is Gran,* he says telepathically. *I perceive that you consider me to be an elf, and this is very acceptable. However, let's just say that if your Earth elves are a prototype then I am the fully developed model. Be aware this is not intended to be a slight on your elves, or even a comparison; it is an explanation only.*

I smile. "I understand. My name is Mixael, and I am honoured to meet you. This is such a delightful surprise."

Gran is slight and slender, yet I can feel an almost tensile strength in him. His features are literally elfin to look at, classically beautiful, but with a sense of presence far bigger than his body. He is wearing brown skin-tight clothing and tiny, supple boots. I mention this only because all the others wear what looks like silk robes of various colours.

Several men and women from my previous 5–D reality introduce themselves. They are all tall, graceful, slender, with an energy of powerful vitality. They assure me that we did not know each other, but they seem as delighted and honoured to meet me, as I feel meeting them.

Finally, the snake-like Being comes to me. Close up, it reminds me of the beautiful Rainbow Serpent with whom I have spent time. It obviously reads my thoughts. She, as she telepathically informs me, is a visitor to this place, rather than a permanent resident. I also learn that at over three metres long, she is able to lift herself so that she is almost upright, with only half a metre of her length remaining on the floor. To me, she is absolutely beautiful with a perpetually smiling mouth.

I appreciate that you do not find me frightening, or repugnant. Many humans are frightened by reptiles. I am connected to the Rainbow Serpent of Aboriginal mythology on your Earth, but in ways that are too obscure to detail.

"Try me, "I say, smiling.

She makes a physical hissing sound, while bobbing her head.

It is about linear time and continuity. Humans are consumed in linear time, while the universe and many of its creatures live in a spherical time frame. You humans all do your best to fit life and history into your linear parameters, but it does not always fit. The Rainbow Serpent is not linear, nor does it live in linear time.

I laugh. "Would you believe I had this conversation recently with Pan?"

You keep highly esteemed company. I felt this energy lingering with you, but was unable to reconcile it with you. I honour you.

I feel a bit embarrassed. "Er . . . thank you. Tell me, do you have a pronounceable name?"

She produces the hissing sound again. *My name is similar to the sound you consider to be our laughter, which indeed it is. However, because you are familiar with the Rainbow Serpent, I would be honoured if you refer to me as Rainbow. My true name is unpronounceable for you.*

May I ask how you come to be here? You are far outside the parameters of linear time—though this is not a problem in spherical time—and you are about to enter a city of the Inner Earth.

I tell them that I am a metaphysical traveller from a future time period exploring life on a deeper level. I mentioned the Great Forest of a different time period I had visited with Pan, and how he suggested that I might wish to see a truly GREAT tree. I keep the explanation as brief as possible. I also mention how the impossibly vast tree had literally inhaled me, and I was suddenly here in this underground place only moments before they found me.

They glance at each other with telepathic knowing.

We knew you had arrived, Staris explains, *because you were drawn in by one of the Sentinels, which is very rare. As this happened, we were told to expect a visitor. Not knowing quite who or what to expect, we deemed it wise that a welcoming committee would need several species to represent us.* She smiles warmly, *And here we are.*

I nod to her. "From my perspective I am bouncing from one shock to another about as fast as I can handle it. I take it that the Great tree is the Sentinel. Just encountering a tree that probably contains more wood and leaves and certainly contains a far greater presence than a whole large forest of my time is staggering. Then to be inhaled into this . . . this . . . er, Middle Earth is incredible.

Staris frowns. *Middle Earth! Why do you say Middle Earth?*

I sigh. "Sorry. Tolkien is a writer of my time, and he wrote a very famous and powerful story about Middle Earth and the Hobbits." I smile. "Maybe he also was a visitor here? I could handle the Hobbits, but I certainly hope you don't have the monsters!"

I'm sorry, I don't understand.

"You don't need to. I'm just babbling."

Are you tired? she asks sympathetically.

I shake my head. "No, not tired, just seriously overwhelmed."

Smiling, she places the palm of her hand over my forehead. I feel a jolt of energy, followed by a wonderful feeling of such deep peace that my inner disturbance vanishes like a mist before the sun.

"Wow! Thank you. I feel fully restored."

As a group we are now walking, floating, moving, toward the amazing city some distance in front of us. It surprises me that deep underground I should see a clear winding stream nearby, with vegetation growing along its banks. Here and there I see enormous cycads, along with species of palms that are entirely new to me.

Gran telepathically catches my attention. *The light of your time is feeble. To us, you live in an era of shadow and gloom, even when the sun is shining. The illumination here is far more intense, thus these plants from a more light-intense era, are able to grow and thrive.*

I'm about to ask how this is possible in solid rock, but it is a rich, damp earth I see them growing in. As we continue, we are moving along a wide polished rock path through a veritable jungle of vegetation, but it is ordered, not wild and random. Such a luxury of flowers is not by chance. I gasp and stop when I see a huge, two metre high orchid in full magnificent flower. I saw one similar to this years ago on Guadalupe, but not with this degree of vitality. Everything here seems to be imbued with extra vigour.

"This is amazing. Do you collect plants from different time zones on Earth, or do some come from elsewhere in the galaxy?"

Staris smiles. *Very perceptive. Mostly they come from different eras of Earth, but you will see in the more planned, and frankly fabulous, botanical parks some that are definitely off-world! We have some time-travelling people here devoted to the plants, so they care for the gardens, collecting and adding to them fairly constantly.*

I smile at her. "This is something I look forward to. Er, could you tell me more about the sentinels? I certainly get that they are very special trees, but are they sentient?"

She glances to her side. *I've asked Gran to answer you. He has a connection with Nature that is unique.*

I will not attempt to explain their actual presence, but it would help if you understand just how much life on Earth has regressed since this era. As you may realise, this period is about twenty to fifty millions of years in your so-called past. Yes, these trees have sentience. Most of them are more than ten thousand years old, and in that time, they have accumulated vast experience of life in its many forms and expressions. The sentinels are in communication with all the higher life-forms of this era. They could well be described as co-ordinators of the higher life-forms, and in some ways guardians, as well as inner-guides.

"To be honest, that we have regressed does not surprise me. When you told me about our lower level of Light, I knew that was not good. Less Light, suggests less energy, and thus less intelligence."

The sentinels have a connection with the Earth planet that transcends all possible explanation. Enough to say that via the Earth they are connected to the whole galaxy. You should also be aware that this connection transcends linear time and space. In this way, we knew of your experiences in the Great Forests. It was inevitable that you would come here.

He smiles warmly. *We also knew of your block to entering Inner Earth. A block which has now been circumvented.*

I am literally speechless with surprise. I have often toyed with the idea of exploring the whole Inner Earth concept, but deep within my psyche I always felt that it was a fantasy, a myth. I have read several books about Inner Earth, but they all differ in various ways. I figured that if the books were consistent this would go some way toward verifying its existence. I visited Uluru to see if I could enter through that huge energy-portal, but entry was denied. Was I denied by the portal, or did I subconsciously deny the portal and Inner Earth? I don't know. Eventually, I gave up on the whole idea of such a visit. It was also at odds with the scientific explanations of our planet. How could there be huge spaces in it? And if there were, why did science not know about them? All in all I created a huge block . . . or I added to the block that was already in place! Anyway, the reality of it really did not matter. I am as I am, and it is as it is! If I was intended to visit Inner Earth it would happen eventually. I was perfectly content with this.

I am not much of a tourist in the physical world. Whether I visit and see a fabulous place, or not, does not concern me. I like to think that I am not a metaphysical tourist either. The spiritual/metaphysical world is of a greater reality, so in metaphysical travel somehow I always seem to be in the right place at the right moment for my soul enrichment. I like this. I do not make regular off-world metaphysical trips for my entertainment. My visit to Mars was unplanned. When the timing is perfect—even if I am not ready or prepared—it happens. I accept this! Not that I have any choice!

"Is your knowledge of me based in the sentinel, or is it based more in your own intuitive connection to other human Beings?"

Once again, I remind you that humanity has regressed. In this timeless time we are far more energetically connected than your people. They are mostly lost in the illusion of separation. He indicates the others with a sweep of one small hand. *We all knew about you and even some of your earlier travels. It is not that we monitor you; it is more that you inevitably seem to throw yourself onto the radar of our perception. Hence the connection.*

"Oh . . . and how do I do that?"

He gurgles with mirth. *It is not intentional. When you telepathically communicate with a Being, invariably you broadcast to all the Beings in the neighbourhood. But you have not yet realised that this very powerful form of communication transcends linear time. By this, I mean that you are speaking to all within your considerable range through all of time, not just the timeline or place you happen to be in. Spoken words lack the energy to do this.*

I feel a brief sense of aggravation. "I'm getting fed-up with being told I broadcast far and wide. I thought that I had dealt with it ... now this! I'll have to learn to manage it once and for all ... and focus."

By now, Staris, Gran, even Rainbow and the others, are laughing. But it is good laughter. No spite in it, just fun ... even if at my expense.

I hang on to my aggravation for a few moments, but in the end I am laughing too. It's a bit like progress through regress. Surely an oxymoron!

It seems we have travelled several kilometres while chatting, and we are now closer to the city. The effortless walk/float is much swifter than it seems, similar to the pace of a medium-fast jog.

The polished stone path is beautiful. It must be inlaid with a huge variety of semi-precious and precious stones, yet the stones energies blend together into a natural harmonic. I get the sense that everything in this ... this place is of a far greater energy than its counterparts in our time. The energy of our stones and plants are lack-lustre by comparison. The flowering plants continue alongside the path with the clear freshwater stream close by. Artfully clever, it is wild and natural in appearance, but very skilfully created. I am seriously impressed.

As we get ever closer to the city, I gasp. I had expected something out of fairy tales, and there is an aspect of that in it, but it is also ultra-modern in its architecture. Or at least, ultra-modern in my time era so far as I have seen and experienced—which honestly, is not much—apart from videos!

"Was this city built, created ... or was it grown?"

Surprised, Staris smiles at me. *Hmm ... impressive. How did you come to that conclusion?*

I chuckle. "Obviously you are only aware of a few of my metaphysical adventures. I watched four specialists and the owner grow a house when I revisited a 5th-dimensional reality. It took a whole day to grow the etheric and astral structure into its place. Then the house matured into a semi-physical reality. Although it is very much greater, this city has a similar energetic feeling. I imagine this was grown long ago."

She nods. *Long, long ago. But we add to it, if or when, required. We make a few repairs and alterations . . . and we added the walkways.*

The walkways are rather like suspended paths; walkways and bridges woven from some material as thick as slender rope, yet obviously of a very high strength. They link one building with another, stretching far over wide paths, small buildings, parks and clearwater ponds, all of which are artfully framed in a riot of flowering vegetation.

The buildings do not appear to have floors or levels, as our high-rise do, yet many of them reach the equivalent of maybe fifty to seventy floors. They appear to be seamless and translucent, with shades of many colours sweeping over the surface in what appears as random pattern. To be honest, I am not a city person, they are too congested and polluted, but this, this is in a league of its own. It is both beautiful and wondrous. The occasional high spires give me the fairy element, while the overall down-to-earth, yet magnificent elegance is simply stunning.

Throughout it all, everything is illuminated. There appears to be no areas of shadow. The illumination comes from the walkways, the paths, all the buildings, the distant walls of the vast cavern, everywhere. In the few books I have read about Inner Earth, they all referred to a central sun. I see nothing of this. Just an illumination that is more powerful than our sunlight, yet without any sensation of burn or damage.

And then there are the Beings I can see thronging in the city. By far the majority seem to be the 5th-dimensional people, while some of them have a more ethereal appearance, maybe 6th-dimensional. Here and there I see giants. Okay . . . very, very tall, but mostly slender. They are not the giants we associate with the word; more like exceptionally tall, slim, people.

There are a number of Beings who are similar to Gran, small and dainty, yet all have that high-tensile type energy. I cannot see any others like Rainbow, although I doubt that she is here alone, or as a species.

There are only a few who are seriously different. One Being who looks a bit like a large, obviously heavy barrel covered in long fur, is trundling along one of the walkways. As it progresses, the walkway seems to sag alarmingly.

I point this out to Staris. "Could the walkway break, or collapse?"

She shakes her head. *No chance.*

"What is it made of?" I ask.

They are made with the silk from our spiders, she replies.

Involuntarily, I shudder. I can only imagine their size!

Staris chuckles. *Mixael . . . are you afraid of spiders?*

"It is not quite so much me, as Michael. He is certainly not comfortable with *big* spiders. I can feel his repugnance and it affects me. We are like a soul amalgam. Even after all this time, his influence is still strong."

She chuckles. *You need to meet Madam.*

"Oh . . . who is Madam?"

One of our big ladies.

"Big ladies?!"

Uh huh, a very big lady spider. We call her Madam because her true name is neither pronounceable nor even understandable. Then there is Madam two, Madam three and so on up to seven.

Oh my gosh! This is not something that I want to meet. Spiders, huge spiders with eight legs and eight eyes all peering at me. Oh god, no. Of course, every one of the Beings is aware of my silent reaction . . . or at least, I thought it was silent.

Staris hooks her arm in mine and steers me over to an area near one of the buildings. *Come, we need to deal with this.*

As when she hugged me, I feel her arm in mine steering me. I honestly thought that when metaphysical I was basically untouchable. She claimed it was the influence of this place, Inner Earth. It certainly has a higher energy.

I'm sure that if I was in my physical body I would either have broken away, or be sweating bullets by now. Yuk . . . spiders!

Hauled along by Staris into an area of natural rock, we soon enter what appears to be a cave within the great cavern. Walking along a passage on what feels like a carpet, I notice with horror that it is woven silk. Suddenly, it opens out into another large cavern. This is the first shadowy area that I have seen. There is no illumination in here, although it is reasonably light by our standards. To my surprise, I see stalagmites towering high in the cavern, with a number of stalactites hanging down. I also see a huge, thick cobweb that connects from one stalactite to another!

I can't do this!

Turning around to make a rapid exit . . . I freeze in horror.

Walking a few metres behind us in total silence is the biggest spider I have even seen. Everything inside me screams to run, yet I stand as though petrified. I cannot move. Not only this, but I am somehow compelled to engage its benign energy. Benign . . . how is this possible?

I am metaphysically frozen in place while its energy washes gently and soothingly over me. How long this takes I have no idea, but it seems to be quite a while.

I understand your fear, but know that I will not harm you. I am a friend of those who accompany you. See my beauty rather than a mind-conjured evil. Feel my true energy, rather than give way to an old, old terror.

As I stare, I feel this calm, peaceful energy flowing over me. Under this influence, I am able to see that she—this must be Madam— is covered in very short fur, with a strikingly beautiful grey and blue speckling all over her. And she is BIG! About the size of a sturdy Shetland pony, her legs in their dense fur appear thick and strong.

Very good. You are relaxing, feeling and seeing nothing to fear.

Her two protruding clusters of eyes move slowly. Each cluster has four eyes watching me. Gosh, even these are beautiful, with shades of deep red within them.

By now, I am no longer feeling the terror of that first glance. Her energy is not only benign, it is engaging, calming . . . and she communicates!

Are you ready to touch me, to push back your boundaries?

My initial terror is receding rapidly. This is not just a spider, this is an intelligent sentient Being who happens to have a spider shape. I think, maybe, that I am ready.

Hesitantly, slowly, Madam moves the few metres toward me. I realise that she is doing this to make it easier for me in this opening contact. She slowly lifts one front leg in my direction, as close to a clear offering of a handshake as is possible for her.

I reach out and lightly grip her surprisingly hand-like foot. It is warm, with a soft flow of energy entering my hand.

"My name is Mixael, and I am very pleased and happy to meet you," I say meaningfully. "You are a lady like none other that I have ever met. Thank you for being so tolerant of my overwhelming fear. I am not ashamed of it, but neither am I proud."

In your time period, snakes and spiders seem to be the embodiment of fear for humans. Each represent the subconscious fear of the unknown, the nameless terror that resides in the darkness of the psyche. You are not the first I have met with this fear, although it is seldom encountered here.

"Yes, it's entirely irrational, but all too common for us."

I hope I am not intruding, but I am intrigued by the two-in-oneness of you. Is this two souls together, or is it the lingering effects of when one soul enters while the other departs?

"You are correct. Our terminology is a walk-in. Michael became spiritually enlightened and deliberately walked-out. It was a conscious decision he made before he incarnated. As part of the same soul-family, I had also made the decision to leave my 5–D reality and re-enter and engage a 3–D reality. I had to both deal with some old emotional issues that hindered my progress and, with many others from a 5–D reality, I intended to offer my skills to assist in the human Awakening now taking place. In this way Michael and I established an agreement between us that if our probability paths brought about that which we intended, or hoped for, then he would depart as a soul, and I as a soul, would take over his body. However, his energy is very powerfully imprinted within his whole cellular structure, so very occasionally a conscious Being is aware of the two-in-one effect."

Remarkable. Thank you for that explanation. As far as I know, this is an ability unique to humanity. And even then, it takes developed souls. Did Michael also have the ability to travel metaphysically?

"Yes. In many previous incarnations he was a wandering mystic, and he suffered very badly for it. In his most previous incarnation he spent his last twenty-five years in a silent monastery. Chant, meditation and contemplation were the order of the day. This is when he strongly developed the skill that he had been exploring as a mystic in earlier incarnations.

"I also had this ability in the 5–D reality, so we were very well matched for the walk-in scenario."

I find it challenging to even imagine.

"To be honest, I found it very challenging. I rather expected to be fully integrated within a year or two. The reality was that twenty years later I was still struggling with it on an emotional level. However, that period of struggle is all behind me now, despite Michael's lingering influence. And I have to say, I enjoy his influence; his humour, his optimism, and his various quirks."

Naturally enough, as Madam engages me in conversation, so my anxiety is ebbing away until there is none left. I feel very comfortable with her now.

"So, is this where you live?" I ask, gesturing into the cavern within the immense cavern. Are you alone?"

I get a sense of pride from Madam. *This is where I live with some of my sisters. There are seven of us who chose to be here to assist the other Beings who live and visit here, in any way that we can.*

And that assistance is both considerable and valuable, Staris adds.

Fifteen

This insight you have shared with us is undoubtedly correct. We have never looked at it quite this way before. My people came here in more recent times, maybe less than a thousand years ago. Each different species offers of itself to the Whole, thus we all thrive. The progress that is possible when all species live in peace and harmony has to be lived to be believed. As a harmonic convergence takes place among us, we all grow in consciousness in the most natural way possible. Struggling and striving comes to an end.

"Are all spiders as big as you, and sentient in this time period?"

No. We are a single species of arachnids who originated aeons ago from far out in the galaxy. Other spiders in this timeline are more like the spiders of your time, although maybe bigger, more robust.

Again I remind you that there are loops in the so-called timeline that make it confusing, Staris says. *Your science seldom makes allowances for anything that is not easily labelled and allocated a place in their linear scheme of things. As I have said, linear time is a human construct, while life lives in a more spherical time frame. There are many examples of where the linear concept of progression is at odds with the all-time-occupies-the-same-moment of a greater reality.*

I nod. "Yes . . . I encounter this quite often. It is disconcerting because even our speaking and our thoughts are linear, so experiences in spherical time are rather difficult to speak about, to write about, or even to think about!"

I feel Madam's energy connect with mine. *You are about to go into the city, so I will leave you now. It has been an honour and a privilege to have met you. I can only hope that you have lost your lingering fear of spiders.*

So saying, she leaves us, moving swiftly and silently further into her cavern. Watching her go, I marvel at her sheer size and beauty. She still looks formidable, but now that I know her, she no longer frightens me.

With Staris, I turn around and walk back through the silken-floored tunnel and back into the vast illuminated cavern once more. Having experienced the non-illuminated place where Madam lives, I expected the Light to appear as rather bright, but it seemed a more subdued Light than earlier. I mentioned this to Staris.

Our city is conscious, sentient and intelligent. Almost every Being gets to experience the illumination at their own level of comfort and perception. We had become used to the far more subdued light that Madam and her sisters prefer, so as we emerged, the illumination made a small temporary adjustment for our experience only.

"That's very impressive. So, all the Beings experience the illumination in their own unique way. Er, just a thought. If I see it as a very pure Light, are other Beings able to experience it in various colours, or just different shades of Light?"

Whatever meets their requirement; brighter or duller Light, colours of a huge range within a much greater spectrum, infra-red, ultra-violet and so on.

I gasp. "And all at the same time, wherever the Beings are! I find this absolutely remarkable."

Although Staris seems to be the main person talking with me, most of the group are still with us. Rainbow departed while we were in Madam's den, but I hope to see her again. We have a lot to talk about. The diminutive Gran is now at my eye level, having effortlessly and easily levitated himself to avoid peering up at the rest of us.

Hmm... neat trick.

We are actually entering the city now, still continuing along the path of polished stone. The stream and its attendant plants and flowers have narrowed down a bit, but they also continue. As we proceed along the path into the city, the path slowly widens to maybe five times its earlier width, obviously to allow room for more people and alien Beings to move along it. Somewhat surprisingly, to me, the accompanying garden has now expanded out in a similar proportion to the path. I am in a city, but I am also in a meandering botanical park with a stream, in the city. I love it!

"When I have read about Inner Earth, I have read of various names for the city that the explorers found. Agartha is one and Telos another, just to mention the couple that I remember. So, do you have more than one city in the Inner Earth, or does each group of explorers get a different city name? I confess, I am confused by this inconsistency."

There are chuckles in the group as I ask this question.

I'm sorry to tell you that you are about to get another different name, Staris says. *This city is named Home. And it is, indeed, our home.*

"Hmm... I like it. Simple and down to earth." I chuckle. "Pardon the pun! So what about the other cities mentioned?"

Agartha and Telos are also cities in Inner Earth, but much bigger than Home and far from here. Most of the cities are linked underground, but not all. Our city, Home, stands unique and alone. We are able to connect with the other cities via entrances from above ground, but there is no underground connection. The structure of Inner Earth does not allow for it.

"So, why live underground, away from the sun?"

*Long ago we lived above ground. We are a long-lived people and experienced numerous Earth changes that brought much destruction to our cities and to Nature, with whom we share our lives. Earlier explorations had discovered huge caverns within the Earth, which we had begun to explore and survey. We eventually discovered that while great changes happened upon the surface of Earth, there was far greater stability within.

For a while we were split. Some ventured underground to build and to live, others remained on the surface. This lasted for several centuries. Eventually, another Earth change was predicted, and we all finally went underground. It seems that our extra numbers of people then triggered a release of energy from within the Earth. We, the people, were changed forever. This included our health, our longevity and our consciousness. We all became totally vegetarian, with fruit our predominant food. It was as though an inner switch in consciousness had been activated . . . and we thrived.

"But you are 5th-dimensional people."

*For us, this came with the switch. With the switch, everything changed. Those few who were unable in consciousness to make the switch were loved and cared for, but eventually they died out. They could not adapt to the new and higher energy.

It is only later that 5th-dimensional time-travelling people from a so-called distant future found us. Many of them stayed here, adding their amazing technology and their skills, delighting in the developments that so perfectly emerged from our shared abilities to build and expand Home. It was they who brought the technology of our illumination. Prior to this, we had lights designed around the flame with clever and ingenious reflection. It was very effective, along with powerfully luminous fungi. But the amazing illumination technology completely transcended it. This enabled us to bring Nature underground. Prior to this, we lived underground but grew our foods above ground, in the sunlight and rain.

"You talk as though you have been here throughout much of this, but that would be ages, a very long time. How is this possible? You are not old enough to have been here for so long."

Staris looks surprised.

Mixael . . . do you not realise that Inner Earth does not exist in linear time? Down here, we live in spherical time. This is the big attraction. Living here we ceased ageing. Or at least, it slowed right down as our natural longevity expanded. We are not sure exactly why time is different here, but it happened with the switch. It is to do with the energy.

I stare at her in astonishment.

"So, this means that your past, present and future are all happening as One orchestrated movement in the moment."

Staris is nodding. *That says it very well. For us, the past is not past, it is fully accessible, as is the future. Both are fully accessible in the conscious moment.*

"Aha . . . conscious being the key word. This suggests, as you mentioned, that living here while less than fully conscious would be very difficult, even impossible. This, in turn means that you do not have any subconscious people/Beings living here. No wonder the energy is so powerful. It is as though a sentient Earth bathes you in a higher energy and each of you reflect it back via the lens of your very living and being. In this way, both the people and the Earth grow in consciousness."

Staris gives me a look of deep respect.

Gran catches my attention. *This insight you have shared with us is undoubtedly correct. We have never looked at it quite this way before. My people came here in more recent times, maybe less than a thousand years ago. Each different species offers of itself to the Whole, thus we all thrive. The progress that is possible when all species live in peace and harmony has to be lived to be believed. As a harmonic convergence takes place among us, we all grow in consciousness in the most natural way possible. Struggling and striving comes to an end.*

"Of course, and in turn this benefits the whole Earth and her fabulous sentinels."

I sigh deeply. "If only the current Changes on our Earth would somehow create a similar result. This would free the more conscious people to create anew, while the many more subconscious people continue along their path in their own evolution of consciousness." I sigh again. "If only."

We are now entering an area in the city where a group of children are involved in some type of game. The children range in age from maybe six to sixteen, but this is a guess. They are all vibrant in health, mostly quite tall for their varying ages, and slim. I should add that these are children of the 5th-dimensional people, for it is they who make up most of the population. I should also add that there is a conformity of tallish, slim, and very healthy bodies in the human population.

The polished stone on which the children run and leap seems to have a thick layer of some moss-like plant growing over it. As far as I am concerned this is impossible. Nothing could grow on polished stone, and also be very vigorously jumped on. The game they are engaged in is reminiscent of our basketball, so there is plenty of leaping action.

I turn to Gran. "This is probably a stupid question, but how can that moss-like plant possibly grow on solid stone?"

He chuckles. *This is just one of the wonders down here. When the game is finished, the plant will roll itself up like a carpet and move over to the soil over there, and continue being nourished.*

"Oh . . . so it isn't actually growing on the stone?"

Not at all. It is there to cushion the fall of the players, thus avoiding skin abrasions, and even broken bones. The harder and higher they jump, or the heavier the fall of a player, the more absorbent the plant is. It is a bit like a natural growing form of kinetic energy. It specialises in absorb and recoil.

"Wow! And it never wears out?"

It is nourished by the soil at the end of every game, thus regenerating itself. So, it never wears out.

As we continue into the city, I am wondering if they have shops here. Or any form of entertainment, like cinemas. So . . . I ask.

Shaking her head, Staris seems to find my question rather amusing.

No cinemas. For pure enjoyment we mostly go above ground into the world of a natural Nature. But this is not an entertainment enjoyment, it is more of a very enjoyable in-the-moment exploration of places of great interest.

She gives me an apologetic look. *You will find that the various forms of entertainment are more for those people who live subconsciously. This is not a criticism, but here at Inner Earth there is no such thing as boredom, or any need to be entertained.*

I nod. "Yes, this makes sense to me. I enjoy my selection of the various movies that are on offer in our timeframe, but I am very aware that I do not need them. So, how about shops? Don't you need supplies for your homes within Home?"

She shrugs. *This is also very different. We do not trade in money or goods, so we do not have shops in the way you mean. However, we do have large Bring and Share areas where you are free to take anything that you need. This includes furniture, food, whatever. The area is large because there are many choices. Of course, the area also caters for our off-world visitors, and our many and varied species who reside here, all with their differing needs.*

I smile. "I find it fascinating that with all your amazing and advanced technology, you are such a down-to-earth people. I like this. I suppose you have no diseases; no physical, mental or emotional health problems, or even sickness in general?"

*No, disease is almost unheard of. Nor do we have the mental or emotional problems. In this higher energy/consciousness they cannot exist.

On rare occasions a person might encounter a problem while on the surface, like falling out of a tree, or spraining a limb in a mountainous area, or even being badly bitten or stung by an insect . . . but this seldom happens.

"Of course, when you are conscious, accidents don't really happen. And if they do, they are not really accidents, more like negligence!"

Staris chuckles. *Very good, Mixael . . . I like your humour.*

I smile. "That, was pure, unadulterated Michael!"

Home is a city like none I have seen before. I have metaphysically visited several alien cities, and cities in different frames of reality and, of course, they are all unique, with many of them also sentient. But Home is such a rich blend of buildings, paths, high walkways and botanical gardens all in such a perfect and complimentary presentation. And, of course, all in a completely controlled environment that creates a very nourishing and somehow fulfilling experience. At least, it certainly does for me!

"Do you have night time here, like when it goes dark?"

Once again, the illumination caters for your wishes. Most of the people prefer to have a night time, so if they go out at night the illumination is simply for their path, to illuminate their passage. All around them it is dark. This also facilitates and maintains our natural sleep cycles. However, another off-world Being might be experiencing full illumination in the same place at the same time, or whatever level of Light they need. It is as near perfect as is possible for all concerned.

She takes my arm once more, steering me toward an area on our left.

This is one of our Bring and Share places. As the name implies, anything that you no longer need, you can bring here for another person or Being. Just as you can also take whatever you might need.

At first glance it seems to be very much in the open and rather vulnerable, but it is surrounded by a dense mass of plants, large shrubs, and trees. I fleetingly wonder what would happen to the bewildering array of goods if it rained . . . but, of course, it never rains here. Or does it?

As I speculate on this, I notice that all the trees are fruiting. They hold an abundance of fruit that I have never seen before, which surprises me. I know most of the fruits, but these are totally new to me. Now I also notice that what I thought of as shrubs are covered in edible berries. And, I realise with a sudden insight, even the plants are all edible. Very clever . . . a constantly growing garden food/store.

Bringing my attention back to the goods on display, I can only guess what the various 'things' are, or what they are for. There are a few obvious chairs, even if slightly strange to look at, and I can recognise what surely must be a number of beds, but while most are flat and obvious, some of them are curved to the side, while others curve upward. Weird!

Hmm . . . I wish I could taste the various fruit, but that's impossible for me to metaphysically manage. And I will never sleep in the beds! So, what was my question? Ah yes, does it rain down here?

I glance toward Staris. "Mostly I have no idea what I'm looking at. The fruit and berries are all new to me, and the goods and chattels are mostly beyond strange. I'm certainly surprised by the size of the area and the amount of stuff, and also by the food growing close by . . . which brings up the question; does it rain down here? I realise that if it does, it would have to be very carefully controlled."

She gives me a throaty chuckle. *You are correct. We do have rain in selected areas at specific times, and it is fully controlled. In this way, we do not have accidental floods, nor do we need them! Moreover, there is plentiful water in the Inner Earth in the form of streams . . . as you see, and in wide rivers and huge lakes. All of the water for the people's needs comes from these natural sources. Interestingly, we have found that for many plant species there is a type of alchemy created when they are exposed to rain. It seems a need for many species, even though they are almost always in moist soil and a perfect growing medium regarding Light and warmth.*

"And that same alchemy applies to a breeze stroking the leaves of many species of plants. Do you cater for this?"

Yes, we do, but plants and a breeze is not common knowledge.

"I'm not a common man," I reply, laughing. "I suppose you have no insect pests, or weeds, or unwanted mould, etcetera."

No Mixael . . . none of those.

"I bet you can grow perfect mushrooms down here."

Would you like to see our fungi farm?

I nod. "Yes please, they are one of my favourite foods."

Continuing along once more, I hear youthful laughter floating out from a fairly large grove of trees. Our path takes us through this grove, and I continue to hear the laughter close by, but I cannot see anyone. Where are the children who are laughing? It could not be the trees, surely?

Gran is close by, so I ask him. "Where is the laughter coming from?"

He looks at me with a sly smile. *Are you unable to see the elfin children? Not all Beings are anchored to the soil. Look up, they are in the trees.*

I stop and stare up into the trees. They look slightly akin to our oak, with broad limbs, wide spread and with a generous cover of leaves. What actually startles me is that when I see the tiny, yet very active children, they are not all standing on the branches!

Noticing my surprise, Gran responds. *Trees are very much a natural home for us. What you are seeing is our children practising their levitation skills. Just as human children learn to walk, our children learn to hover, or levitate. And if you look carefully, you will notice a home in the tree you are peering into. Do not look for big clunky furniture for big clunky bodies, look more for subtle indentations and carved curves in the branches of the trees.*

With a sigh, I levitate up into the branches with the children. Most of them shriek in a mixture of surprise and glee, but from above I can see exactly what Gran means. There are subtle areas in the branches where they have been carved and polished, reshaping them into various differing contours in which the diminutive bodies can relax. The thought of me attempting to physically relax on solid polished wood holds no appeal. I like to recline on something soft, but these are very different Beings.

Obviously, Gran heard my thoughts. *You have already realised that our bodies are not soft, like human bodies. Imagine very strong and very flexible bone or rubber, and you have an idea of our physical construction. We are almost impossible to break. We could fall from the top of the highest tree, then get up and walk away.*

He holds out an arm to me, and although I am metaphysical, by touching his arm he conveys to me exactly what he meant. It is a bit like touching surprisingly warm spring steel. No wonder I sensed high tensile strength in him. As small as he is, a human would have no chance in arm wrestling with one like him. Small and fragile, they are not!

I am also impressed by the sheer unworldly beauty of the children. Eyes that are slanted, and so deep a green as to be almost luminous in their intensity, these elfin people are an extremely attractive and vibrant species.

I deliberately share this telepathically with Gran, and he smiles at me with delighted appreciation. So many Beings have almost frozen features, but these elfin Beings have facial expressions that easily communicate their deeper feelings. I feel very attracted to them.

We continue following the polished stone path toward the fungi farm. Now that I am no longer a novelty, but more of a boring tourist, a number of the other people have drifted away to pursue their own interests. Now, with Staris and Gran, only a couple of other people remain.

Our path takes us into an environment where the illumination is no longer so dominant. It casts a much reduced light into a large, very moist area. The whole atmosphere has changed. I guess it would be regarded as rather swampy by modern standards, but without the accompaniment of clinging mud and biting mosquitos!

"Is this a deliberately created environment?" I ask Gran.

He nods. *Yes, the underground water is close to surface in this place, so we designed it for growing as wide a range of edible fungi as possible. Some grow directly in the moist soil, but most are grown on old logs, growing trees, rocks, in moss and lichen . . . and so on.*

Leading me from one area to another, he showed me how the different species had their differing needs met. Some required greater illumination, others less. When I was last in Japan, I saw many varieties of 'mushrooms' in the street markets of old Kyoto, but never in my life have I seen as many as there are here. Hundreds, maybe thousands of varieties thrive in their own specific environs all within the large area designated as the Fungi Farm. And colours! Some are bright yellow, some ghostly white, some a startling red, while some are even a luminous green, growing from moss beds!

I chuckle. "I really enjoy quite a variety of mushrooms, but ours mostly all conform to a pale greyish or brownish, even blackish colour. I would be seriously challenged to eat a red one, or yellow . . . and green, yuk!"

If you did manage it, you would be dead in moments. Many of these are highly toxic for humans.

"So why grow them?"

Gran regards me patiently. *Mixael, we cater for many off-world species here. What is toxic for us is a delicacy for some of them.*

"Hmm, yes. I forgot about that. We have a saying; one man's meat is another man's poison."

Staris nods sagely. *You would not forget if you lived here. We are all very different. Some of our off-world visitors do not breathe oxygen in the way that we do. For some, methane is the main requirement, with a tiny amount of oxygen. A few require a far higher percentage of oxygen and far less nitrogen than us, and so it goes.*

"I understand that the illumination can change according to the various needs, but don't tell me the atmosphere can as well?"

No. There are certain districts in Home that cater specifically for off-world needs. You will see that those with special needs all wear a tiny pack and breather with the perfect mix of gasses that they require.

As we walk among the various fungi species, I see that some trees with very thin leaves are growing horizontally, rather than vertically. They are almost flat to the ground, yet growing vigorously while covered in fungi.

I point to them. "They cannot be regular Earth trees, surely?"

No, they are a symbiosis brought here by some off-worlders. So, we grow the fungi that those particular off-worlders most enjoy. Nor are they the only ones. The luminous green fungi grow in a very specific moss that does not naturally occur on Earth. Yet, when introduced, they all grow and thrive in the conditions of a controlled environment.

Impressive. Very impressive.

"Okay, so where do we go from here?"

Staris gives me an enquiring look. *This depends on how much longer you will be with us.*

"Strangely, I feel more fatigue in my physical body than I do in this metaphysical body. I suspect that this is to do with your timelessness. I am intrigued by the idea of underground lakes. Do you have any that we could visit?"

She nods enthusiastically. *Oh yes. We have a botanical garden and lake all in one beautifully landscaped region. We will visit there . . . and relax.*

Continuing along the stone path, we take one of the many paths where it branches off from the main avenue. I should mention that as we have walked along, the path has forked off into many different directions, which we mostly ignored. Now we follow one such path, still polished stone but slightly narrower, toward the designated park and lake.

Hmm . . . like it or not, I can feel the familiar signs indicating that my return to physicality is imminent.

I smile at Staris. "It seems you are right. I will not be with you much longer. So in case I suddenly disappear, thank you all so much for your wonderful hospitality. I deeply appreciate it. I will be back, somehow! There is so much more to see and learn."

This time, my withdrawal is slower, considerably less abrupt. I realise as they all progressively fade out, that it is I, who is fading away . . . to gradually become aware of my physical world once more.

I feel a deep sense of loss.

Sixteen

I and others of my kind have dropped in on various tribes from time to time. We are known by them. They hold a certain ... reverence, for us as we have assisted them on several occasions.

A MONTH PASSES BY, gardening and reading.

The sense of loss lingered longer than I expected. It was not based in the people or any one person, it was the loss of a certain higher frequency of consciousness that is no longer with us. Indeed, we have regressed a long way since that long ago time.

The *why* of our regression intrigues me.

I understand that life is cyclical, but I am also aware that life was designed to be in cycles on an *ascending* spiral. Human life was never designed to be cycles on a *descending* spiral as is happening. Why is this?

I have a different view of life in my holistic world-reality. If you have a question, you also have the answer. You cannot have a half of a whole in a holistic universe. The question is in the left-hemisphere of the brain, which sees through the eyes of separation. The answer is in the fully connected whole-brain, balanced and holistic.

The question is in intellectual words, the true answer is not. Truth is a living holistic experience which, more often than not, cannot be mentally intellectualised. It may be emotionally felt, but then we seek to understand the emotion . . . so off we go on yet another tangent. We seldom accept that our emotions are a non-intellectual language with nuances far beyond the intellect's ability to understand. By attempting to mentally understand our deeper emotional language, we reduce our emotional sense of the world. We have done this for so long that we now believe this reduction to be normal.

Sadly, most people do not trust their emotions. They do not trust decisions made from the heart, or from their intuition. We have an education system based entirely in the development of the left-brain intellect. And the left-brain will never understand our intuition. This is not a left-brain function. I clearly see that our whole basic educational system has severely reduced us. I am sorry to say that for me, this was undeniably its purpose. We are intellectually clever, while holding hands with stupid. War is an example of stupid! There is nothing of intelligence in warfare.

This is not an *ascending* cycle of intelligence. Whole-brain development and an educational system based around this would have produced a very different humanity by now. I could take a chapter to explain all this from a metaphysical viewpoint, but that is not what this book is about. This book is about exploring the holistic and timeless world we live in to <u>experience</u> our answers, rather than intellectually chase them down the lonely avenues of illusion and separation.

Growing in consciousness; it's the only <u>real</u> game to play!

Christmas comes along . . . and passes.

The New Year, 2023, unfolds.

It is cool in our subtropical region and drier than I prefer. Rain would be very welcomed by our garden. I like Christmas well enough, but the usual process of buying gifts for family and being given gifts by family has become senselessly institutionalised by the commercial world of greed. And as soon as the New Year is a month old, the supermarkets will be selling Easter hot cross buns. Ridiculous, but profitable.

Our greedy, fearful way of life creates its own energy. It is not a bad or wrong energy, but it is a greedy and fearful energy which pervades much of humanity. Certainly not all. This, in turn affects the whole human frequency. If you so choose, growing in consciousness will lift you above this. Then fear and greed lose their hold on you. But how can you rise above it if you think that this fear-based greed energy of consumerism is normal?

This is just one tiny aspect of our regression. In so many different ways we have lowered our overall frequency without realising it. I have felt it more acutely since I metaphysically travelled to that long ago time. I hope to revisit the Inner Earth Home in our current timeframe . . . if it is still there! I would like to meet with Gran and Staris again. And Rainbow and I have much to talk about, but I imagine they are long gone in our present time. Who knows? Time and life seem to consist of endless loops and many surprises.

* * *

I decide one day that I will metaphysically follow the timeline for the formation of the small mountain ridge on which I live. Obviously, there are times when the Earth is in upheaval, landscaping on an epic scale—I suspect that this has happened far more often than we realise—so this is a period I need to aim for. Perhaps I will learn why I was so strongly attracted to eventually live here. It could be that the city of a higher frequency is the attraction. I do not know, but I suspect it is not. It was such a total unknown. Maybe I have had previous experiences on this ridge? Thirty-six years ago life made it very clear that this was to be my home. I remember when we moved in, our elderly neighbour, Ruby, told us that if the mountain liked us we would not be able to leave it. And if it did not like us, we would not be able to stay. I am still here, despite attempting to move away a couple of times, so obviously the mountain likes me. One thing is clear, for whatever reason, the energy here is higher, finer and more powerful than the surrounding areas.

Sitting back in my study-chair I relax. This is where I have written many of my metaphysical travelling books, so the Study energy is mostly primed and ready . . . when I am!

As I gradually allow my focus to expand into my metaphysical body of Love and Light, I move into an altered state of consciousness. There is no here or there, All is One. There is no now and then, All is One. The real world of a greater reality reveals that the physical world we live on and believe in, is a holographic image that shapes itself to our thoughts and beliefs. When we have almost eight billion people with varying beliefs, religions, anxieties and endless fears, then the holographic Earth becomes less stable. Earth itself is a vast elemental consciousness, with both intelligence and awareness. In a greater reality there is no fear, no anxiety, no belief in death, none of our illusory nonsense of endless issues to be dealt with, and so it is for Earth itself. Despite this, Earth *is* affected by our fears, our greed, our poverty, sickness and suffering. It is not so much a negative affect, and most certainly not a positive one, but the Earth *is* affected.

I have a focus that I will follow with regards to the mountain ridge, yet I am open to allow that which may intervene, or intrude, or even turn me aside. It is as it is. I go where I go!

*   *   *

I step . . . Between . . . realities, moving my aware focus away from my physical body and into the greater Whole. This metaphysical travelling is a consciousness thing, not a physical skill. We believe that consciousness is anchored in our brain; it is not. *We are consciousness*, not brains or bodies. Intelligence does not need a brain through which to operate, it operates via consciousness. We operate our brain in accordance with our consciousness.

So as I consciously move into the All that Is, I hold a gentle focus on the mountain ridge. I metaphysically rise upward, well above the rocky ridge, allowing me a greater view. It is my intent to go back in time, yet I realise that forward or back in time is all part of the illusion in which we live. I have found that the more I have learned and know, the more I am able to allow that which IS to emerge. Human learning and knowing is so often unwittingly holding hands with beliefs, ignorance, and limitations.

Beneath me the landscape is very slowly changing. It is my choice to follow the regression of the ridge via biological, linear time. Even knowing this, I am surprised to see the mountain ridge growing taller and wider. I had forgotten about the impact of millennia of erosion. Fancy, my small mountain ridge was once quite a big one! Of course, while this is happening the whole area is going through some quite dramatic changes. The coastline is moving out to sea in undulating movements . . . and then receding again as the rock and sand shoreline is forever changing.

What was a scattering of trees when I began, this has become a thick forest, and this also gradually fades to far less trees than we have today. I am seeing faster change than I anticipated. The climate is also going through change. Climate change! There has never been a time without it. Sometimes slow, sometimes much faster . . . like our current times. All this is a constant factor of growth and change on Earth, and life adapts.

My mountain ridge seems to have stabilised, not growing any bigger. It is now about twice the size of the ridge I live on! Both higher and wider, I did not expect this.

Sitting in the lotus position about a hundred metres above the mountain ridge, I am startled to see a Being approaching me through the airways as though fast walking on a stable path. Hmm . . . *very* fast walking!

Within moments, standing in front of me is Seine. I am filled with joy as I gaze upon my magnificent friend. Seine is a feline Being of great beauty. A bit under two metres tall, slim, totally feline with short, dense golden fur, he truly is splendid to behold. An old friend, we travelled and explored much together, before I eventually got lost in the human illusion.

Leaping to my feet I embrace him, feeling his firm body against mine.

"This is such a wonderful surprise," I tell him.

Unlike Earth felines, his eyes are round, like two silver orbs of mystery. Almost disconcerting, it is as though I am seeing an ivory moon peering at me through his eyes. He blinks, and a filter slowly moves over his eyes from the side, then rapidly vanishes. Although his energy is masculine, he is sexless in his higher dimensional body.

Welcome, Mixael. Would you like a guide and companion?

I laugh. "Would I ever! Nothing could please me more. This is a bit like old times."

Those times were when you were the 5th-dimensional Mixael. Now you are a 3rd-dimensional Michael/Mixael. Yet, since I was last with you, there is less of Michael and considerably more of Mixael.

I laugh. "Well, that's nice. It's interesting: as I grow in consciousness, I am aware my growth also affects Michael. Equally, as Michael grows in consciousness, I also grow. We affect each other in ways I did not expect. And I have no clue where or when he is. Not that it matters."

I pause. "So . . . how did you know I would be out here?"

Seine smiles. *You are a beacon of Light to which I am attuned.*

"Gosh!" I feel very humble, very honoured.

He smiles easily. *Do you have any idea where or when you are going, or is this an exercise in meandering?*

"As you know, I live in the 21st century on that mountain ridge beneath us. I consider it has a rather special energy, and I am intrigued about why, and if I have had a prior relationship with it. It's all a bit vague, but I feel it might be important."

Seine chuckles. *So . . . an exercise in meandering.*

I nod. "Purposeful meandering."

Together, side by side in a lotus position, we watch the centuries roll past. The change beneath us is not so pronounced now, even though the coastline continues to expand and recede.

What do you think that is? Seine asks, pointing to an area I judge to be close to my home. When I first came aloft, I took particular notice of a few prominent landmarks in case I might need them. As I look to where he points, I see a light a bit less than a kilometre from where I estimate our house and garden to be. What the light is I have no idea.

"How far are we in the past, do you think?" I ask Seine.

A question to a question, he smiles. *About twenty to thirty thousand years, I would say.*

"Hmm . . . I have no idea what the light is, but it might pertain to the higher energy on the ridge in my time."

Straightening up, we sink quite swiftly toward the mountain ridge.

As we get closer the light is growing stronger, rather than brighter. It is not overly big, but neither is it very small. From a distance it seemed to be about the size of a very small dwelling, but as we get closer it looks more like a strongly glowing very large box.

"This is weird!"

Finally, we come to Earth, quite close to the box-like structure. Now that I am close, it seems to be made of some glass-like material, with the light coming from within.

I must admit, I am equally puzzled by this. It makes no sound, it has no obvious means of propulsion, yet it is a powerhouse of energy.

"And it's on my mountain ridge in this coastal wilderness."

Standing totally intrigued, I am suddenly aware that we are not alone. I now hear a single voice chanting in a strange, guttural language. As I look toward the place where the chanting is located, I see an aboriginal elder staring fixedly at Seine. But he is not the one chanting. He is one of a group of around eight men of the First Nation. They are all staring at Seine as though in shock.

"They can see you, but I think my metaphysical body is invisible to them. Maybe they associate you with the light, or whatever-it-is!"

Talking in what sounds like an alien language, Seine slowly approaches the men. As one they drop to their knees, bowing low. Keeping an eye on them, I go over to the light box. Reaching out, I tentatively touch it. Although nothing physical could burn me, it feels as hard as steel and cool to the touch. In its energy I also feel something for which I have no word, no name, no clue, yet I feel it connect with me.

Only now do I realise that while touching the light, the natives can see me. How this works, I have no idea, but it is obvious by their agitation. The man who was chanting now emerges from the bush, still chanting. Old, yet sprightly, he is painted with a whitish resin, standing bold on his almost naked black skin. He exudes a savage splendour with an undeniable dignity.

Walking slowly toward Seine, he replies in that same alien language. I stare in utter amazement. A First Nation medicine-man and an alien feline Being are easily communicating and understanding each other.

"Don't tell me you know each other?" I ask weakly.

Listening to the witch-doctor, Seine communicates telepathically with me in our usual way. I seldom hear him speaking aloud, as he now is.

I and others of my kind have dropped in on various tribes from time to time. We are known by them. They hold a certain . . . reverence for us as we have assisted them on occasions. Even though we are both using a spoken language, the real communication is more telepathic.

"Ask them what this light is."

I have done so. They say that it came gently to Earth long ago, and that very slowly it is sinking into the rocky ground. I estimate this to be over a period of maybe a hundred years. The people of this tribe gather here about once a year to give the light their blessings. They tell me that in this process they are healed of sicknesses and septic wounds. They are concerned that the light, which was once much bigger than this, will eventually disappear into the rocks and earth.

"Incredible. There is no visible light there in my time, so it must have sunk deep into the mountain ridge. Maybe it's still descending. I wonder what it is, and why this is happening."

They consider it to be sacred . . . and friendly!

"Yes! I get it. When I touched it, I felt an energy coming from it that I could not identify. *Friendly* describes it exactly. I didn't even think of it in those terms. Wow, I'm seriously impressed," I reply excitedly. "No wonder the energy of the mountain ridge is so powerful . . . and it likes me!"

I smile in delight.

So is this the end of your meandering quest?

"No way! This is just the beginning, even if my meandering will now be a bit less purposeful. Who knows what may turn up next!"

We both give a slight bow of respect to the people of the First Nation before we once again rise up into the sky. They watch Seine ascending with a look of awe. Maybe his likeness is to be found in some of their rock art!

I honestly did not expect to get such a clear and definite answer to my enquiry about the mountain ridge. Interestingly, the light seems to be located in the beautiful property that today is owned by the Meher Baba Foundation. Occupied by some of the devotees of Meher Baba, they lovingly maintain the delightful property. Having spent several past incarnations spiritually connected with Meher Baba, since his transition he and I occasionally meet. I enjoy his wisdom, overlaid with his abundant sense of humour.

"Maybe if we stay in place, we will see the arrival of the light. That would be interesting."

A few more centuries pass by, the coastline continuing to expand and shrink, but we do not see the approach of the light.

Is it possible the light turned on only when it reached the Earth? We are waiting for a light to come from above in an alien artefact. Possibly it did not happen this way. It is even possible the light was a beacon to attract rescue.

"Even so, surely we would see a box or whatever as big as that if it came down and crashed below us. Hmm . . . we solve the mystery of the energy of the mountain ridge only to encounter another mystery as to how it got there."

Even as I speak to Seine, we both see a large object falling from the sky while spinning over and over as if out of control. A light flashes from it intermittently.

"Oh . . . wow, look at that. Mystery solved. Er . . . should we follow it down and see if we can assist?"

I agree, we will. However, Mixael be aware that your Michael aspect is very impulsive. Please do not do anything that we may both regret.

I sigh. He sounds just like Pan! "Message received and understood."

As we follow the mysterious object down, we hear the surprisingly minor crash of its impact. When we arrive moments later, I expect to see a small crater, but instead the object is already slightly embedded in rock. It looks more as though it has grown upward to emerge, rather than having crashed downward to be eventually engulfed.

"No wonder the crash sounded so faint. It cannot be very heavy."

I think it is more the nature of the object. There are substances to build space-faring craft that are unknown to your civilisation. Very lightweight and virtually indestructible. Some are literally grown.

"I get the feeling that there is nobody inside."

Yes, I too get a strong feeling that it has no passengers.

"Surely it should be glowing red hot, having come streaking from space into our dense atmosphere. Yet I'm standing close to it and there is no heat at all. What do you make of that?"

He smiles. *You are talking about the physics known to the general public of your time. Far superior alien technology has already been shared with some governments, but the public know little to nothing about this. Secretive governments do not willingly share such information.*

I nod. "Yes, this all makes sense. However, I would like to correct you about our civilisation. We are <u>not</u> civilised. We treat people and nations and different skin colours and cultures appallingly. We have almost zero tolerance of others, and our governments lead the way with their lies, corruption and deliberate control of the people. Sorry, but we are still in kindergarten as regards civilisation."

Seine smiles at me. *But Change is upon you.*

"Yes. The death of the old energy, and the birth of the new energies are taking place simultaneously. And long have we waited."

I have a sudden insight. "I wonder if this artefact is deliberately planted like a seed to burrow into the Earth and, at a certain time, to be triggered into releasing an energy that will assist in the birth of our new Golden Age. This would also explain why there are no passengers. Suppose this is not an accident at all, but a purpose . . . along with others like it scattered over the Earth. All unknown. Think about it. The light came on permanently when it reached Earth. Who knows the qualities of this light? The aboriginal elders described it as friendly. I agree. Maybe we could also add . . . Loving!"

Seine gives me an admiring smile. *You are basically correct. I would not have told you, but your intuition is powerful. Remember, nothing by accident.*

I feel elated.

"Why wouldn't you have told me?"

Because I encourage your own journey of enquiry and discovery.

"Gosh . . . I am so glad that I decided to explore the timeline of our mountain ridge." I voice my earlier thought. "Are you an emissary of Pan, by any chance? You often seem to act in that role when he is not around."

He laughs. *No Mixael, I am not an emissary of Pan. However, I am a very long time friend of yours, and I am doing all I can to bring you back to the powerful awareness that you once had. It is not something that is lost; it cannot be. But it has been buried in the illusions of your 3-D world, and disrupted and distorted by the control of the low consciousness overlords.*

I feel indignant. "They are *not* overlords, they are a few corrupt families who share a draconian bloodline and obscene wealth . . . and control."

I agree. A good description of the overlords. But do they not lord it over the mass population?

I sigh. "I suppose if you put it like that, it makes sense. But for me and all people like me, they are absolutely *not* my, or our, overlords. And they never will be. They have no Light or Love in their hearts."

My words trigger another insight.

"It is possible that these artefacts that have so deliberately burrowed or sunk into the Earth, will create a global network of light? This is a light energy that will connect with all those people who have their heart-light switched on by consciously, choosing and living Love."

I pause. "Something like an ascension beacon that connects with all those who are focussed on growing in consciousness. What do you think about that for a conjecture?"

Seine has a broad smile on a face designed for smiling. *I think that your intuition and perception is re-establishing itself very nicely.*

Seventeen

As you know, humans are a two-in-one package. There is the physical body living within physical laws, and there is also the metaphysical Being living within a multidimensional reality. Attempting to understand with the physical brain the metaphysical Being that you truly are, is always going to be limiting. The path to higher knowledge is not only via the three dimensional limits of the intellect, but also through the far higher reach of the holistic whole-brain/heart connected intelligence which is boundless, limitless . . . and available.

"Okay, Seine . . . you have been my companion in this little jaunt. Now how about being my guide, as you mentioned earlier?"

Or even your mentor?

"Why yes. But the role of a mentor is to teach, surely. You encourage me, but you do not really teach me."

I am offering, right now.

"Why now . . . so suddenly?"

Timing, my friend. It is all about timing.

"So . . . you're saying it's time?"

Do you think it is?

"I think this is a ridiculous conversation. I am happy for you to mentor me any time you think I need mentoring."

Good. Listen carefully. How do you metaphysically travel?

I smile. "I step between realities."

So . . . what does this mean, exactly?

"It means that I step between realities."

We already ascertained this. But what are these realities that you step between? Where are they located?

"Er . . . what?"

Explain these different realities to me.

I sigh. "Okay, let's say that life is made up of endless frames of reality. They are rather like pages in a book. Each page is a different reality yet they are all bound in, and connected, in the One book. So, I found a way to step from one page to another."

Very clever. So, what does this mean you are?

"Seine, I have no idea where this is going. I don't even understand the nature of the question. It means I am capable. How about that?"

Yes, you are undoubtedly capable. No argument there. We will try another angle; what is the whole basis of your spiritual teachings?

I frown. "Okay . . . In every moment of your life you are creating the direction and content of every moment of your life."

Very good . . . and very correct. But this is not the teaching to which I am referring.

"Okay . . . but there are lots of them. So, you tell me which one you want, and then I'll tell you."

I'm sorry my friend, but this is important. Be patient. Think about it.

Sitting in the lotus position high above my mountain ridge, I think deeply about my teachings. Which is the most fundamental one? Is there one thing that I say over and over? As though it's become a Michael quote.

I think long about the separation aspect of humanity, and the holistic viewpoint of a much bigger picture. Ah yes . . . I think I have it.

"I teach . . . there is nothing outside Self."

Seine smiles delightedly. *That's the one. So now consider my question once more. If there is nothing outside Self, where are the many different realities to be found?*

Hmm . . . an obvious trap. Or is it? "Okay, I have never looked at it like this before. However, the obvious answer must be, the many differing realties are all within Self."

Yes . . . wonderful. So, what does this mean that you are?

Oh gosh . . . here we go again. "I'm sorry, but I don't get it. How does this make me anything?"

Please continue to be patient. Think deeply. You teach there is nothing outside Self. So when you metaphysically travel, when or where are you going?

I sigh, long and deep. I am clearly being guided or pushed in a certain direction. When or where am I going? I never really know until I get there. Hmm . . . going to, getting there! This suggests a place, a destination. But where? Hmm . . . nothing outside Self. Oh! So, there is nowhere to go, no when to go . . . outside of Self. So, what does this mean I am? Oh!

"Are you suggesting that this means . . . I am a gateway?"

He laughs. *Finally. The word I had in mind is 'portal.' You are a portal. This means that anywhere or any-when you need to be or go, you are the portal of that time or place. There is nothing outside Self. No other realities, no other worlds, not even universes. You are all that is. Obviously!*

I nod, quiet and thoughtful. "Wow. I feel I have just been kicked in the butt. My world just got bigger. Amazing, my own words, yet I had never fully embraced them. Certainly not to this extent! If there is 'nothing' outside Self, then I am it. All of it. Of course, this is the magnificent, metaphysical, multidimensional Self. The immortal, eternal Self. The Self that is a Being of Love, the power of creation. And a Being of Light, the illumination of eternity."

I sigh. This is the Truth of all humanity, of each person, not just my truth.

This is our potential. This is what our spiritual journey slowly reveals. Our material games within the illusion simply hold us in denial. We each live so lost in the personal self and the physical world of want and need that it takes almost endless incarnations to finally move into the Light of Truth.

"It reminds me of the adage of a water drop in the ocean. The single drop 'is' the ocean in the drop, while also being the drop in the ocean. If the ocean is all that is, then so is the single drop. Nothing outside the ocean!"

It was all within your consciousness—the timing—but it had not yet fully revealed itself as Truth. This is due to the Michael influence. His many incarnations of experiencing the pain that accompanies separation take a long time from which to recover.

"So everywhere I have ever metaphysically visited is all within Self."

He nods. *All within Self . . . that vast field of energy/consciousness that represents every living thing in the universe. When you finally know and acknowledge Self as a portal, then metaphysical travel takes on a whole new meaning. We are holistic Beings, so why should metaphysical travel be less than holistic?*

"Why indeed? My world just got a lot bigger."

Actually, no. Your view and appreciation of the world just got bigger.

"Whatever. It's strange how some of the greatest discoveries we make are about that which we already know. Or thought we knew. And yet that which we know is but a thin slice of a whole huge cake. We know the crumbs, but not the whole cake. In fact, the cake seems to not even exist in our current crumbling reality."

I smile.

Clever . . . but reasonably accurate.

"Okay . . . so where are we going now?"

How will it affect your metaphysical travel is the appropriate question?

"Hmm. It seems to me that when I stepped between realities, even though I was obviously a bit deluded about it, nevertheless I was the unsuspecting portal within which I stepped."

A fair enough comment. How will it be now that on a higher level you inner-know that there is nothing outside Self? Will it be more of the same, or a new way where you need never over-jump your target?"

"Oh my gosh . . . how did you know about that?"

Word gets around.

"You mean gossip gets around. Fancy, you listening to gossip! It's not easy leaving a place to which you have an emotional attachment. It throws all your calculations out the window."

Seine just patiently smiles at me.

"Okay . . . so will you stay with me?"

Consider me tethered to you.

"Suppose that I don't have a destination. What happens?"

Focus on nowhere and nothing and find out. However, I should add that it is a good way to get lost!

"Really! I don't like getting lost, especially when physical. But to be fair, I very seldom get lost metaphysically."

Out of pure curiosity, I focus back about a hundred million years. No need to step anywhere . . . because as a portal, I am both here and there simultaneously!

Using a photographic slide as a metaphor, the mountain ridge fades out and an ocean fades in. We are hovering over what appears as an endless, boundless ocean.

So . . . the point of this is . . . ?

"I have no idea. I just focussed back a hundred million years. I guess we are in the same place. So, the point is pointless."

Try again . . . and please, give your destination substance and meaning.

Chastened, I have to agree.

I think about it carefully. I would like to revisit Home, in the Inner Earth, but about a thousand years later than my last visit.

Again, the photographic slide fade-away from the ocean and the fade-in as the widely scattered sentinel trees appear once more.

The sun is very clear in the sky, the atmosphere almost sparkling with intensity.

Ah . . . the sentinel trees. Destination Inner Earth, I presume?

"Yes. A thousand years later than my last visit. My gosh . . . is there any place or time you don't know?"

In truth, they are beyond numbering. Forgive my asking, but why not enter from one of the legitimate entrances?

"I don't know where they are."

He smiles at me gently. *Mixael, they are all within Self. You just focus on exactly what or where you want, and the portal you are will open into that place. It is all within your connected consciousness.*

"Oh . . . that had not occurred to me. Sorry, I'm a bit slow on the uptake. But of course, it makes sense. Hang on!"

I focus on an easily accessible entrance to the Inner Earth of this time. And just like that, we are there. In front of us, there is a deep slit into a steep rocky hillside. It is, however, a very remote sort of place.

Turning to Seine, I gesture toward the entrance. "Ready and waiting, sir. Shall I ring, or will we enter unannounced?"

Seine laughs out loud. *I have no doubt at all that we are already well and truly announced.*

Together, Seine and I walk toward and into the slit in the hillside. It is narrow and cobwebby, as though people seldom ever come this way. As we move deeper into it, a vast cavern is revealed. It is dark. Metaphysically, I can see in darkness and it seems no problem at all for Seine. Nevertheless, I am surprised by the deep gloom, I expected illumination.

By way of a joke, I call out with telepathic strength. "Let there be light."

Instantly, a familiar but faint illumination throws the shadows into disarray.

"Wow . . . I didn't expect that!"

I am impressed.

"Hmm . . . but this is not as bright as before."

It is then that I become aware of the carpet of webbing that covers the floor of the cavern. "Oh my gosh! I think we have come in at the wrong entrance!"

I see movement coming toward us from several directions, and with a gulp of shock, I recognise them as huge spiders. One moves out ahead of the others, heading directly toward me.

As she approaches, I see the beautiful blue and grey speckles of her short fur . . . and with a sigh of relief, I relax.

"Er . . . is that you, Madame.

Yes. Welcome back Mixael. We did not expect to see you so soon.

"So soon! This is a thousand years later . . . or it's supposed to be."

She regards Seine. *I see you keep illustrious company.*

I am flabbergasted. "Oh my gosh . . . don't tell me you know each other!"

Seine smiles at her. *It is a pleasure to see you again, Madame. I had no idea that you and Mixael have met.*

Oh yes. I was a serious challenge for him about a thousand years ago when he suffered from acute arachnid-phobia. His reaction this time is a great improvement.

When she replied to Seine, she projected her words to include me.

"Madame, did I come in the wrong entrance?"

Not really. But when you visited us last time, you did not notice that, considerably deeper in the cavern, is our exit and entry when we leave here to go foraging outside. You came in there.

"Oh. Er . . . how can you still be alive a thousand years later?"

You are measuring linear time. For we inhabitants of Inner Earth, linear time does not exist . . . except when we go outside. A thousand linear years is a passing moment for us. You need to realise that all time occupying the same moment is a mere concept for you, while it is a living reality for us.

"So, are Staris and Gran still here?"

I have not heard of them leaving, so most probably, yes.

While we are talking, Madame's sisters have gathered around us. I am happy to realise that I do not feel threatened by their close proximity. They all have the same coloured fur, but even so they are not quite identical. I think it is mainly an energy thing, but for me, Madame is unmistakeable. She is also slightly bigger than the others, more strongly built.

"If you point us in the right direction, we will go and surprise the others."

Actually, I doubt that will happen. They, like us, would be well aware of your approaching presence, so they may be waiting to surprise you.

I laugh. "I look forward to seeing them."

While walking and chatting with Seine, Madame leads us quite a long way through various caves and tunnels, through areas of stalactites and stalagmites all bearing huge rope-thick cobwebbing, and yet all within the cavern of her domain. Everywhere we walk is on the carpet of spider silk. Eventually, we reach a tunnel that feels vaguely familiar to me. As we walk along, the intensity of light grows gradually stronger, and finally we emerge onto the polished stone walkway I previously walked.

Thank you for using our entrance, Madame says, *it has been a pleasure to meet and talk with both of you again.*

So saying, she moves back into her cavern once more.

The illumination is considerably brighter once outside the complex of the huge spiders. I look around, almost expecting to see a welcome committee, but we appear to be alone.

"I didn't realise that you have been to Inner Earth," I said to Seine.

As you might expect, in my many millennia of travelling this section of the universe, I have been to places, times, and destinations beyond count.

I nod. "Of course . . . when you put it like that! You know, I like the name of this place, Home. It is simple, yet somehow profound. We have a saying: 'Home is where the heart is.' From the moment I first visited, this place and my heart were united forever. In many ways, this feels more like Home for me than any place in any incarnation that I remember. I love where I now physically live, but not in the way I feel about Home."

I hear a chuckle of approval from above me, and looking up I see Gran grinning down at me while reclining on the wide branch of a tree, as though in an easy chair.

Close by, stepping from behind a large flowering shrub, a smiling Staris says, *This is your Home also, whenever you wish it to be.*

I laugh. "Madame said you would be nearby."

She embraces Seine. *Hello, old friend. You, I did not expect. I knew that you and Mixael are long-term companions, but I did not know that you were together until you arrived in the cavern.*

Another back-door entry for our new friend.

"Okay Gran, you will have to show me the front door, complete with the gold-plated knocker. Then, maybe, I'll get it right."

It feels good to be Home. In my metaphysical travels, I have encountered many places where I would like to spend an incarnation or more, exploring and experiencing the wonders of life beyond the illusion. But Home, and the lure of Earth all this time ago, is very appealing. If the vast and incredible sentinels are any indication, there is so much to see and experience above ground, as well as below.

After embracing Gran and Staris, I ask Seine a question. "I thought that I really understood how all time occupies the same moment. And I do, to a certain extent, but I am realising that much of my understanding still remains conceptual. Coming back here a thousand years after I left, and finding all these people so fully involved in their lives without ageing a single day, is very confronting. Even the plants appear the same. However, energetically I feel the growth in consciousness that has taken place here, there is no hint of stagnation whatsoever. It is the same with you. You are an ageless Being, yet always growing in consciousness. Would you mind further explaining this timelessness to me once again? I really want to fully comprehend it."

As odd as it seems, Mixael, this long ago past is far out in your current future. This is one of the ambiguities of linear time. Do not confuse linear time with your Gregorian calendar. You have had other calendars before this, along with the more complex Mayan calendar. A calendar simply attempts to make linear time more manageable for people. Linear time is a design to create cause and effect, polarities, duality and repetition as teaching tools. However, this does not mean that it spirals endlessly into the future. It does not. It loops and twists according to the universal needs of the eternal moment. While linear time is being measured off second by second, hour by hour, year by year in your time reality, it is also reflected in the biological ageing of Nature all around you. This makes linear time very real. You have living proof. But just as your people are not physical Beings in linear time, but are metaphysical Beings in a greater metaphysical reality, so is all Nature, all life. You learn, and spiritually grow using the tools that consciousness has supplied, thus you gain an ever deepening comprehension of life. You are designed to eventually see through the teaching-illusion once it is no longer needed. You, Mixael, have done this, as have many others of your timeline.

I smile, as I feel a deepening comprehension flowing into me.

"Yes, being faced with timelessness, with eternity, is challenging, but enlightening. I need not understand it, but I struggle to, nevertheless."

You need to realise that the brain of 3-dimensional humanity is wired to understand 3-dimensional reality. That which you do understand mostly falls within the natural laws of physicality. That it makes sense is important. Physically, you live within the rules of physicality. However, you are also a metaphysical Being of Love and Light. As you know, humans are a two-in one package. There is the physical body living within physical laws, and there is also the metaphysical Being living within a multidimensional reality. Attempting to understand with the physical brain the metaphysical Being that you truly are, is always going to be limiting. The path to higher knowledge is not only via the three dimensional limits of the intellect, but also through the far higher reach of the holistic whole-brain/heart connected intelligence which is boundless, limitless . . . and available.

I stand quietly, letting his energy of deeper knowing sink in.

Sighing deeply, I nod. Rather than fully understand it, I feel it . . . and it feels very good . . . more whole.

"Thank you, Seine . . . the timing is perfect."

Staris has been listening to Seine, nodding in agreement. Now she looks at me enquiringly. *It is wonderful to see you again, Mixael, but why have you returned so soon?*

I laugh out loud. "So soon! It is a thousand years later! How can that be, so soon?!"

Staris smiles. *And there you have it. No years for us, but a thousand years have passed in linear time. And for you, how many years for you?*

I stare at her, shocked. "Oh . . . wow! You are right. I have come here a thousand years later, but only a few months for me. I never *fully* realised that linear time could be a destination, rather than an all-inclusive reality."

Well, it is real that a thousand linear years have passed outside, but for us they have not, neither have they for you where you live. So what is real?

I stare at her in surprise. "What indeed? And to answer your question, I came back a thousand years later to see for myself how timelessness affects reality. What I have learned is that the question, what is reality . . . has no *real* answer in reality! How strange is that."

*   *   *

A few timeless hours later, I depart via the portal of Self. Following his own agenda, Seine stayed with them. He planned to catch up on old times and renew old acquaintances.

Eighteen

Do you realise that what you think can literally become the lens of your perception? Logic and established beliefs strongly suggest that for you to see the Earth so far away, it must be beneath you. You did not even consider the possibility of it being above you.

I HAVE A LOT to think about. For example, it was a bemusing thought that the Inner Earth I visited was many millions of years in our past, yet via the inconsistency of linear time, it is also in our distant future. One day in the future, will I be living in the city of Home? I would like that. Is this why I felt so fully at home there? My future Home in the past! Would my Inner Earth friends be there also? Meta-physical travelling completely trashes linear time. It all seems very clear and understandable while I am metaphysically involved, but when I get back to my physical life in linear time, it is no longer quite so clear-cut.

This, alone, offers a considerable feast of appetising speculation.

Add to this the light that Seine and I encountered. Personally, I am sure that it is this, more than anything else, that contributes to the energy on our mountain ridge. I like to think that the living city may also contribute, but that is within a much higher reality frequency, and I am not aware of any seepage. But the light, along with the Meher Baba Centre being exactly where it landed and bedded down, makes a lot of sense. I think Meher Baba chose the area himself. I seem to remember that it was from photographs, but I am not certain of this. He proclaimed that the area had a very high energy, and this would be their centre for the southern hemisphere.

I'll ask him for more details the next time we metaphysically meet.

I am also rather busy, both experiencing and writing this book, plus creating and pre-recording modules for my teachings online. This, and a dozen other things that always need doing in the large garden. Add to this the input from Carolyn, "Michael, you should do this, it's important," or "Michael, will you please come here for a second?" Which actually means, 'Michael, come here for as long as I need you,' all keeps me rather busy. I'm sure you get the idea . . . especially if you are married! Despite this, as far as I am concerned, I am in a dream marriage, with one of the world's most radiant, loving, and caring woman. I am blessed beyond all measure. There is absolutely nothing I would change in my truly wonderful life.

* * *

One day, surprising me on returning from the garden, Pan suggests that together, we embark on a different view of the world. I am surprised because usually it is I who asks for Pan, or it is I who instigates new travels into whatever Mystery attracts me, or it is I who suggests just a time of cosmic meandering.

"Thank you, Pan, I appreciate it. I would love this."
Good. Make ready.
"What different world view do you wish to show me?"
I have no wish to show you anything. I but make an offer.
"Okay, okay . . . I freely accept the offer."

I have long known that Pan does not easily tolerate me putting my own interpretation on his words . . . which I do all the time! I have to if I am to write these types of books! In our conversations he will point it out when he considers that I have been presumptive in my interpretation . . . as I was just now. Then I often get quite brusquely corrected. When I once, rather smugly, suggested that he need not sweat the small stuff, I got quite a long lecture on the fact that there is no small stuff. Stuff, he said, whether it appears as small or large, is all our human translations of energy manifestations, and that we seldom get our interpretations correct.

What could I say? Ah well, I do my best!

I make ready.

Having no idea of a destination or even why, I focus on connecting with Pan, and step through the portal of Self.

* * *

I am somewhere in space hovering over the planet Earth. Naturally enough, I am alone, but I feel Pan's energy is with me. Okay, I am not alone. I am in space accompanied by the mystical, enigmatic Spirit of Nature.

What do you see?

The truth is Pan knows exactly what I see, or am seeing. However, for my own benefit, he mostly gets me to describe it. And, I admit, it works. All too often what I am seeing is my own personal interpretation of what I am looking at . . . and I am wrong!

"I see the Earth quite a way beneath me. It is beautiful."

So, you see the Earth beneath you?

"Yes, I told you that."

Indeed you did. However, the Earth is far above you.

See what I mean? I am wrong again! But, as usual, I do not give in without some sort of struggle.

"Isn't it possible that my location in proximity to the Earth is all an illusion? Down-under or up-over is all a matter of interpretation."

I inner-feel a deep laugh. *Nice try. Now, stop looking at, and truly see with your full metaphysical depth of perception.*

To the best of my ability, I deepen my little-used sense of perception. By little-used, I mean in my normal daily life. Very few of us make a decision to consciously develop our intrinsic sense of perception.

"Okay . . . I agree, the Earth is far above me. But if it is this way, then where I am located?"

Do you realise that what you think can literally become the lens of your perception? Logic and established beliefs strongly suggest that for you to see the Earth so far away, it must be beneath you. You did not even consider the possibility of it being above you.

"I agree . . . even though I have never realised this. Right now, it becomes glaringly obvious. Lesson learned, thank you."

Despite your best intention, the lesson is not yet learned; it is revealed.

I nod. "Yes, I can accept that."

Are you ready?

"For what?"

What is not important. Are you ready?

I sigh. "Yes, I'm ready."

It seems as though space momentarily blinks . . . yet nothing further happens.

The Earth is still spinning in space, but I think it may be further away.

What is your proximity to the Earth now?

I focus with unbiased perception. Despite what I am supposed to have learned, the truth is, I have absolutely no idea of my proximity to Earth.

"I'm sorry Pan, but nothing seems to have changed."

And do you know why that is?

"No."

Because nothing has changed.

"Oh. But . . . but, it seemed as though space blinked."

It did. But nothing changed. You, in your onslaught of speculative thinking, thought that something must have changed. Else, why the blink? However, as stated, all is as it was. Actually, you did surprisingly well in this. I did wonder what you might conjecture. But you chose humble honesty. This, among other reasons, is why I mentor you.

"Oh. Er . . . thank you." I feel both humbled and gratified.

Remember, when you are in space, you have nothing familiar with which to orient yourself. In a physical reality you are orienting and reorienting yourself constantly, even though this has become a subconscious process of which you are mostly unaware. For what I am teaching you, I am taking away the markers you normally use. In a greater metaphysical reality, when, and where, are no longer markers, for when may be where, and where may be when.

I nod. "Yes. I have had a little experience of this."

Earth is still spinning far above me . . . I think.

Where is the sun?

Oh gosh, I have no clue. I seem to be hopeless at this.

"Pan, I'm confused. I no longer know whether the sun is above me, or below me. To say that your lesson is disorienting me is putting it mildly."

Can you see the sun?

"Yes, no problem with that. It is the *where* that I have a problem with."

Please, answer me. Is the sun above you, or below you?

I sigh. "Okay, the sun is above me."

Good, you are correct.

"That's all very well, but to be honest, I don't have a clue about why I am correct."

I feel that familiar inner chuckle. *You are correct because the sun is above you.*

"You know that's not what I mean."

Consider carefully, why did you choose the sun is above you?

Hmm . . . now what. Okay, he said 'consider' not think. And I did not think about it. I 'felt' it was above me.

"Intuitively, I felt it was above me."

Excellent. You went to a higher source of Self than old beliefs and old knowledge. You chose to trust your intuition, despite the pressure I was putting on you.

"So to put it metaphorically, I switched channels. I switched from my inadequate intellectual knowledge, to the intelligence of intuition.

Exactly. The location of the sun is irrelevant in this exercise. I was encouraging you to switch channels *as you elegantly describe it. In space, in the astral worlds, in a greater metaphysical reality and, I must add, in your daily life, intuition is, indeed, the underused quiet voice of intelligence.*

"Thank you. I think *underused* is the operative word. Although I consider myself to be quite an intuitive man, it is all too easy to forget that it is, in fact, the voice of intelligence. My years at school were few compared with a full education of today. Since then, I have had time for life and a greater reality to educate and influence me toward deeper insights. So many of the kids who leave school nowadays are literally locked into their intellect, and effectively locked out of their potential intelligence. Happily, despite this, the older souls can never be denied access."

"So, what is next on the agenda?" I ask, flippantly.

You *are still on the agenda.* You *are what the agenda is all about.*

Pan's reply demonstrates how quickly he can erase flippancy!

It seems that once again there is a cosmic blink, and the Earth is now perfectly framed in my vision. By this, I mean the Earth fills my vision, but it is still an out-in-space vision of Earth.

"How can space possibly blink?" I ask.

It does not. I am the blink.

"Oh my gosh! I am way out of my depth."

Depth is the key word. You are not out of your depth. We are creating more depth within you. We do not create inner depth while you remain in your comfort zone, so you are spending time out of it. This . . . hopefully, will create a greater depth in your inner perception of life.

"I have to admit that this does makes uncomfortable sense."

What do you see on Earth?

"I was hoping you would ask, because it seems as though the Earth is sprinkled with sparkling lights. However, they are far outnumbered by what I can only describe as dull lights. There are radiant lights, and lights that glow dully. But, there is more. In clusters, there are lights that are more anti-light than they are light. They seem to swallow light, rather than shine light."

This is a surprisingly accurate summary. What does it suggest to you?

I think and feel very deeply into what I am seeing. I allow both the voice of reason to make suggestions, and the intuitive voice of intelligence.

"To me, the lights represent humanity. The radiant lights suggest people of a higher consciousness. A greater light is shining forth in a small, but reasonable percentage of humanity. The very many lights that are glowing, but dull, suggests that the majority of humanity is still clinging to the old consciousness. They are resisting the rising wave of energy that is now strongly sweeping Earth. I feel that the clusters of anti-light people are directly opposed to the growth of human consciousness. I feel that these are both the controllers, and those who knowingly and willingly work for them. Interestingly, their lack lustre energy-fields seem to subdue the light of humanity. I am glad that they are in the minority."

This is a reasonable summary. Now I would like you to give me an in-depth account of the people of radiant light.

"Er . . . I just did."

That was an overview. You are allowed to move. There are no rules saying that you cannot approach the Earth, or even interact . . . within the frame of 'look and learn' rather than your usual 'touch and meddle.'

"Oh . . . I can interact? So . . . er, what will you do?"

Do you really want me to answer that question?

"No, no. Sorry. I'm feeling just a bit overwhelmed."

Then, go. It is said very gently and lovingly.

I need that gentle and loving change in energy. I feel as though I am involved in tough end-of-term exams. Ironically, I consider humanity is facing end-of-term exams, after a very long and tough period of lessons! I thought that I had already done mine. Hmm, no room for any sneaky complacency in our growth process.

Hovering in space far from the Earth, I focus on the people with radiant light. Then stepping through the portal of Self, I ask that I am able to connect with one of these people.

* * *

I am in a noisy room filled with a small, but rowdy crowd. Some of them are swearing mildly at the speaker, who I now briefly notice on a platform facing the crowd. As I gaze around at this totally unexpected scene, I wonder if I have made a huge mistake. I smile to myself. Mistakes do not accompany Pan and me. Look and learn . . . this is the rule.

My attention is drawn to the speaker. I thought at first it was a man, but in this modern world, women also wear trousers, or slacks in the modern jargon! I gasp. She is radiant. She has a light strongly emanating up to three metres from her physical body. Metaphysically, she is large and powerful. But, of course, these people just see a slightly built, rather cute young lady.

As I stare at her, sympathising with her for the hostility of the crowd, she catches my eye. Okay, not quite my eye, but she focusses on me. She is clearly aware of me. Her surprise is evident as her words falter. Immediately, the crowd becomes even more rowdy.

Smiling at her, I send her the most powerful boost of Loving energy support that I possibly can. To me, she literally radiates stronger than ever. Interestingly, as her energy floods over the crowd, I see people catching a look at themselves from her viewpoint. Some of the people appear shamed. A few, the most belligerent ones, mutter to their friends, and slink out of the room. A silence settles over the crowd. Slowly, it becomes an audience of about sixty people, no longer a small, unruly crowd.

She continues with her talk about Global Change through Unconditional Love. Okay, this is a subject close to my heart. Walking unseen through the room, I approach the platform to be closer to her. Her eyes follow my progress, with no break in her flow of words. I stop when she is within the radiance of my own field-of-energy. Clearly, she is now feeling even more empowered.

I listen to her speaking, deeply moved by her passion, her energy and her surprisingly deep insights into life.

There are no more interjections. The disturbing and unruly element has either departed or, hopefully, is actually listening. I notice a few men and quite a few more women with tears glistening on their cheeks. The energy of the speaker has filled the room, enfolding the audience and increasing the light in most of them. A few resist, but silently!

I must have appeared in the initial stages of her talk, for she continues for about an hour, or so. When she finishes, a hush descends over the people. One person begins clapping, and is immediately joined by the whole audience. She smiles at them, nodding happily.

As a speaker myself, this is a scene with which I am very familiar. I stay and wait as the people trickle out of the door. Some hug her, some hover, not comfortable with hugs, others grab her hand and pump it enthusiastically.

Finally, the room is empty except for the young lady and myself.

Looking directly at me, she speaks. "Thank you so very much. With such a poor reception I was about to give in, but as you appeared, I felt my energy growing and expanding. I knew then that I would be okay. May I ask, who are you? Are you one of the illumined star people?

I am not physical, so I have no physical voice. I test her with telepathy and, although surprised, she responds well to my explanation. I tell her that I am an older man named Michael living in Australia, and that I practice metaphysical travel. I also tell her that I have been mistaken for an angel a few times, even for God, but this is the first time as an illumined star person.

She quickly settles down to our conversation. I tell her why I am there with her. I also tell her *she* is one of the radiant people . . . and we need all we can get.

I do not go into long and involved explanations, it is not necessary. So, after telling her it is time for me to depart, I allow her the last words.

"As far as I am concerned, whether you agree or not, I consider you to be one of the illumined star people. I am honoured to have met you."

"The honour has been mine," I whisper in her heart . . . and I leave.

* * *

"Wow . . . that was different. Nothing like I expected. She was just a lovely young lady with an incredible radiance of Love energy. "Blessed are the Peacemakers," for that is what people like her truly are."

I share in-depth about my insights of the one radiant person with Pan.

"Do you want me to approach others, or is this lady enough for you?"

Is this enough for you?

"Actually, she is enough. I think more will simply be variations on the same theme. They truly are radiant. I read from her field-of-energy that she has a few personal issues just like everyday people, and she may well have relationship issues, but that is all about being human. It is the issues that teach us tolerance, compassion and, eventually, unconditional Love."

I feel approval from Pan.

"So, I guess the people of dull light are next? This time, rather than a single person, I will aim for a group, or gathering of such people."

However you feel it to be appropriate.

Although I am not at all sure what to expect, nevertheless I focus on a group of the people with the dull light, and step through the portal of Self.

* * *

Immediately, I am standing in a room within another group of noisy people who are all speaking and shouting at the same time. There is no speaker. Not sure what is going on, I connect with the energy of a quiet young man, hoping that I can read the energetic pattern of his energy field. I hope to learn what the agenda is of the rabble . . .

because this is a rabble!

Apparently, this is a protest gathering.

The main aim of the group is to protest over the cloud-seeding program they have been researching. They are angry and aggressive. According to their research, all sorts of toxic and mind-control chemicals have recently been distributed from high altitude aircraft over the cities and countryside. When I metaphysically look for the dominant emotion of this group, it is fear. Fear, the one emotion that is completely counter-productive to their plans and intentions.

It seems no one is taking a leadership role. Each person wants everyone to hear about *their* research, and to be aware of *their* anger at what is taking place. The result is a rabble, shouting, arguing, and swearing about those who inflict this crime on humanity.

I sigh. I can entirely sympathise with their feelings of hostility, but the hostility is all personalised. They speak and shout as though this is an affront aimed at them, personally. Of course, none of them are aware of me, or my presence. The quiet young man is exuding defeat. He can see that this is not going anywhere, but he has no idea what to do about it.

I decide to try an experiment. Unseen and unrealised, I make my way into the very centre of the mob. Then, I consciously radiate my Love/Light to spread throughout the group, so that they are all within my field-of-energy. I smile at the result. Imagine a fire-blanket thrown over a fire. As long as the blanket covers the flames, it will quickly smother the fire. This was the effect. My Love/Light includes everyone, and the noise, the anger, the shouting all drops very fast.

Suddenly, they are all looking at each other, a bit shame-faced.

One of them coughs, apologetically. "Okay people, we need to get a bit of order in here. This is supposed to be a meeting to ascertain what we can and cannot do about the chemtrails. Seems it's turned into a shouting match instead."

He comfortably took further control. "Okay, as chairman, I call this meeting to order. I will ask Marge, our secretary, for a brief rundown of the minutes of our last meeting. Each of you who have duties, get up on the stage and into your seats. Let's get this meeting underway with no more shouting."

And so they do.

I smile. Love triumphs once again.

* * *

I then step through the portal of Self with my focus on a single person who is a dull light. He is a middle-aged man, walking along the pavement in the city. He is in no hurry. He looks wealthy, with expensive clothing and shoes. This is obvious even to me! His features reflect his inner feelings, a very unhappy and angry man. Life is incredibly unfair.

After several years of an affair with a younger, vivacious woman, his wife had been informed. Even worse, someone sent her a brief video of him and Veronica. His wife was furious, and was filing for divorce. That was okay, but she was suing him for every dollar she could lay her hands on. So bloody unfair. And she was taking the kids. She was no longer into sex as often as him, yet she denied him going elsewhere. He told her he loved her, and she told him that actions speak louder than words.

As he walks along, his thoughts and accompanying emotions are like a storm of negativity. Dominant among them . . . fear. He is heavily mortgaged to maintain his and her lifestyle, and a divorce payout will financially ruin him. And she does not care!!! You should have thought of that earlier, she said. Such bloody ingratitude!

I leave him. He is not about to become a radiant light anytime soon.

* * *

In the same city, on the other side of the road, three dull lights are walking along together.

I move over to them. Three, very serious, twenty-something girls.

Reading their fields-of-energy, I learn that their landlord has given them notice to vacate the flat they share. Or, they could pay a much higher rent. Far above their financial ability, this is not an option.

These are good people. Basically, they are victims of greed.

Once again, the dominant energy is fear. And understandably so. The city has a high level of homelessness. Rents are going up everywhere, as uncaring and ruthless landlords cash-in on the misfortune of the people.

What can I do? I am here to look and learn, not give greedy landlords a metaphysical beating! So, once again, moving into their midst, I radiate my Love/Light over the three girls.

"Hey, come on. We're not going to be beaten by one greedy louse. I have a few contacts, and I bet each one of you do also. Let's be positive about this and just *know* that we are going to get the perfect apartment at a rent we can afford."

And just like that, they are brighter lights once more. I knew that with this new, positive attitude, they would find what they were looking for.

Time for me to return to Pan.

*   *   *

"One thing is certain," I tell Pan. "For many of the dull lights, it is a temporary thing. Equally, for some it is a permanent marker. Or, at least, for this lifetime. I also have learned that my first perception of humanity as radiant lights, dull lights and anti-lights was a bit simplistic. There is a huge range of human light energy in-between all that. Nevertheless, these three categories of light are the fundamental markers of human energy.

I told you to look and learn. You have been meddling. You empowered the single speaker, you calmed the energy of the rabble, bringing order, and you turned the energy round of the three girls. Why did you do this?

I am astonished. "Since when has it been a crime to help people with a simple application of Love energy?"

It is not a crime. It is not wrong. It is not bad. Look and learn means that you observe, you do not participate. Is that so difficult for you?

I scowl. "Well, obviously it is. Look and learn is all very well. But would I physically stand on a river bank and watch a person drown, simply because you told me to observe? No, I would not. I would be true to my own nature. I would dive in and do my best to rescue them."

Mixael . . . although I feel that this is a Michael lesson! Within physical life everything you see and experience around you is the manifestation of a greater metaphysical reality. If you save a person's life, or end it, you are now an aspect of their own outworking. Naturally enough, cause and effect are involved, and there will be repercussions. But on this physical level, those repercussions are comparatively minor. However, when you are in a greater metaphysical reality, you are in the very nucleus of life. You are within its higher frequency. You are not in the lower physical outworking frequency of this. Do you understand what I am saying?

I nod. "Yes. The metaphysical precedes the physical. I think I can see where you are heading with this."

When you strongly influence the probability-template of a person, minor as it may seem, you have basically changed the probability of the person's template, even their life, maybe forever. This involves you in a way that connects you with the new template that they create.

"Is this so bad?"

This has nothing to do with bad or wrong. It is all about responsibility. Do you really want to be responsible for the probability template of people you do not know?

"Pan, in all my metaphysical adventures, both with and without your direct influence, I have affected the lives of many people on a metaphysical level. Why, suddenly, are you bringing this to my attention?"

Because I wish to protect you.

The sheer energy of his words suddenly changes from powerful and compelling . . . to a soft and loving energetic caress.

To say that I am shocked is putting it mildly.

I am speechless, brimming with emotion as I stare at the Earth from my position in space.

Timeless, eternal, beingness.

Eventually: "I'll go and see what I can learn from the anti-light people. And seriously, Pan, I will do my very best to observe without participating. I never deliberately disobey you. It just seems to happen."

I inner-hear/feel the faintest of sighs.

Taking a deep metaphoric breath, I focus on an anti-light person and step through the portal of Self.

*   *   *

I am in an executive Board Room. This is obvious. It is at the top of a high-rise building, in a room that exudes wealth and simple luxury. There is a huge, plain, solid, but very beautiful polished-wood table dominating the room, with twenty, red upholstered, very comfortable matching chairs around the table. Fifteen of them are occupied. The overall energy in the room is like nothing I have ever before encountered. It is corrupt, malignant and hypnotically controlling. In a word, evil.

One person, a woman, is standing. She is speaking to the others. As I observe the energy of the people, I realise that although they look to be in their forties and fifties, energetically they are all about fifteen to twenty years older. Strange! The speaker is dominating most of the other people with the sheer depth and energy power of her words. She is an anti-light person, as are three of the others. One on her right, two on her left. These three anti-light people are all men. And dangerous.

I realise that I have, literally, jumped into a hornets' nest.

I can feel the energy of the four anti-light people as a tangible force to be reckoned with. Powerfully negative, compelling, almost irresistible. In all my life, I have never encountered anyone like these four. The others are more in the category of sycophants. Forceful in their own way, with a dominant energy field, but also boot-lickers.

They are not a threat.

I notice that the eyes of the four have flickered over me. Never making and holding contact, but they are aware of my presence. This is not good. As it happens, all of them are within my own field-of-energy. Clearly, they have registered my arrival.

There is a rapid build-up of hostility, of negative excitement from them.

I feel a human force of malevolence, an evil gathering of violence just waiting to be unleashed. On me?

Hmm . . . what do I do? I can make a rapid retreat, this is one option. I can wait and see what happens, but . . . ! Or, I can engage them on an inner energetic level. Which is exactly what Pan told me not to do!

Oh dear. Why do situations like this happen to me?

Abruptly, I am out of options.

I am shocked when I feel a whiplash stinging across my metaphysical body. The pain is intense. Good grief, what is happening? With the totally unexpected metaphysical pain of the whiplash, I am deeply confused. Then, another whiplash of pain assaults me. I instantly know this comes from a different man. For some reason, this time the pain brings clarity. I am in a fight. They started it. They are attempting to control me, maybe even kill me.

Instantly bringing my Love/Light up to full power, I allow it to fill my field-of-energy. Good grief, I am being attacked for the very soul I am.

It feels as if ropes of foul energy are also thrown over me, attempting to bind me, thus reducing my energy field. I become rapidly aware that these three men attacking me are very adept in the dark arts, using their esoteric knowledge to try and bind me to their will. Or kill me.

Oddly, I now feel calm and confident. I am Love. There is no power greater than Love, the Power of Creation. This is my focus. This is the foundation of my divinity. I am unconquerable. I am Love.

I neither fight them, nor fear them. The brief moments of shock and fear have passed. I am shining Light. I am radiant Love. I am unassailable.

A timeless struggle takes place. Because they are the ones who are struggling, one by one, two of the men give up. The man on the right of the woman—who continues talking in the Board Meeting as though nothing unusual is happening—is no longer attempting to control me. He is now definitely trying to kill me.

I watch him as his face tightens with the effort. I continue watching as his face goes from a strained white to very red . . . and then to purple as he continues to fight and strain against the Power of Love. There is incredulity etched into his distorted features, as though he cannot believe what is happening. Rage, hate, and sudden fear flare in his eyes.

It now occurs to me that it is this attack Pan was hoping to protect me from. Oh my gosh, this was in my probability template, and he knew!

There is an unexpected and loud gasp, as the breath explodes from the last man who chose to attack me. His body shudders, and his head falls heavily forward, his face smashing into the polished surface of the table.

His life energy abruptly fails. He is dead.

The Board Meeting unceremoniously ends. The people not involved in the metaphysical struggle jump up and rush around to the body. One grabs his phone, calling for an ambulance. The woman speaker glances in my direction, a look of demonic hate distorting her features. She also looks pale and shocked that he could be defeated.

I did not defeat him. He defeated himself.

Lesson learned, it is time for me to depart.

* * *

I am calm as I wait for Pan's expected and forceful reprimand.

Instead, all is silent as I feel his energy lovingly enfold and embrace me.

"You saw all that took place as a strong probability in my timeline template, didn't you? And you tried to protect me." I say quietly.

Again, my emotions surge with the intensity of gratitude that I feel.

Yes. It was an experience that I attempted to circumvent, but it was so strongly imprinted in your probability path, that the confrontation was inevitable.

"I'll be honest, I feel no guilt or blame whatsoever."

Mixael, you are as blameless as the flame that consumes the errant moth. I came on strongly to you about the earlier experiences so that, just possibly, you might avoid the encounter, but as I said, it was inevitable.

"I don't understand. How can you, the Spirit of Nature intervene in the affairs of people? You never do this. Never. It is against your very nature."

No words. Just Pan's loving energy embracing me. "Oh . . . I just remember. I am an exception. In that time before this, when I metaphysically melded with my developing embryonic forerunner, it was you who intervened to free us. That moment was unique. It created an energetic connection with you that I have carried through every incarnation ever since. Am I correct?"

No words are necessary. I *know* I am correct.

"I have to admit, I was totally shocked when the first whiplash attack came. Shocked and confused. And the pain was intense. Yet, now, nothing.

What happened to the pain?"

It began with the three men trying to control you. When two failed, as you surmised, the last man attempted to kill you. He has killed often with his dark arts. Mixael, you were very impressive. You did everything perfectly. You stepped into your power, your Truth, and in this way you were unassailable.

"He killed himself . . . like the moth with the flame. I was the flame."

Exactly. Had you engaged in fighting him, you would have lost.

"Oh. Why?"

Because the moment you engaged him in fighting, you would also have engaged fear. His skills were based in fear and dominance. He had never before battled a person who did not fear him. So, he had no idea of the consequences of throwing all his dark skills against Love. He ruined his own heart in attempting to stop yours.

"And the pain?"

The metaphysical damage from the metaphysical attack was healed by Love. However, you will probably experience mild physical repercussions.

"Pan, I am very grateful that you tried to circumvent this encounter for me, but with me following my own nature, it was already assured."

All is well that ends well.

"I certainly hope that it is ended. Is it possible that they could follow my metaphysical trail with their dark esoteric knowledge?"

Had you fought with them, and survived, they could have followed your energy trail. Because you did not, Love left no trail for them to follow.

"Wow! Like the song says, Love changes everything! Er . . . is there anything else I should do? Like, more lessons?"

I feel the inner smile of Pan like a miniature sun. *This will be all. You have been involved in an encounter that was far beyond anything you have faced before. And you handled it admirably. In truth, you dealt with it beyond all expectations. You held back Michael's natural aggression, following the only solution that held a positive outcome for you.*

As you rather aptly described it: you have passed your end-of-term exams . . . with honours.

"Thank you. Except, of course, my term with you has no end."

* * *

With a smile, I return home.

Epilogue

FIVE MONTHS LATER.

About a week after the metaphysical attack by the dark adepts, I began to struggle. My health was on a downhill spiral. To be honest, at first I did not make the connection between their attack on me and my downhill descent, but gradually it became ever more obvious. I confess, I refused the doctor-hospital-prescription drug system, trying in my own way to understand what was happening to me. As I indignantly said to Pan, this is not a *mild repercussion*, it is a huge and savage one! He then told me that there is a reason behind everything.

So it was, that I continued to spiral into a deep dark place. A place of pain, bone-jarring aches, vomiting, and fatigue beyond belief. I lost 12 kilos, becoming a shadow of the robust man I was at 85. I hoped by the time my 86th birthday came in April, that I would be recovering, but alas, the day came and went while I was still exploring the abyss of pain, despair and suffering.

With Carolyn, I visited a local therapist in Noosa, who has had twenty-seven years of experience with a Mora Machine. The MORA therapy is a holistic diagnosis and treatment using a probe on 40 acupuncture points on the hands and feet, and the bio-resonance Mora machine determines where there is inflammation or areas that are out of balance.

Once these areas were determined, and through the use of the machine once again, the appropriate homeopathic remedies, of which there were hundreds, are tested and narrowed down to which one(s) achieved a balance for any organ or system that was out of balance. Those remedies were then fed back into my system through the probes as an electronic application through the acupuncture meridians. As far as I am concerned, it is this machine and others that will supersede it, that are the future of our medicine.

Apparently I had three lines of attack within my body: a viral, parasitical and bacterial infection that had been in place for many years. This was the gist of my health problems. I had the Coxsackievirus that affected my throat, sinus, chest, cough, pancreas and immune system. Along with this I had rickettsia, a bacteria affecting my nervous system . . . which trashed it. And, as though this was not enough, I had a cryptosporidium parasite causing vomiting, weight loss, fever, and liver stress. These three together, and the inflammation they created, were the basic physical cause of all my symptoms. My immune system was heavily compromised, thus putting a huge strain on my liver and pancreas.

The metaphysical attack somehow triggered the final collapse of my immune system, fully activating the dormant virus, bacteria and parasites to suddenly thrive. I felt like death warmed up.

It eventually reached the stage where I could not function. I was in pain whether I was sitting down in a chair or lying down on my bed, so I had to resort to painkillers. I took the mildest over-the-counter ones I could find. Oh God . . . what a relief. I could finally sleep. I could get out of bed and walk upright . . . for a while. Two painkillers when I went to bed and two around midday. It did not change my situation, simply masked it, but they afforded me much needed relief from the endless, relentless fatigue and throbbing pain.

Through all this, Carolyn was wonderful. She nursed and cared for me with a devotion I had never needed or experienced before. My daughter Tracey took care of all the potted plants, the hanging baskets, the orchids, everything that needed regular attention in and around our large garden. My family and friends all rallied around doing whatever they could to ease my burden. I was/am very blessed. The Amigo's, Henry and Bruno, came every week to either work in the garden or to chat with me. We had some very deep and meaningful conversations while sipping on coffee. I, however, completely lost my taste for coffee, becoming a drinker of fine teas.

But why was this all happening? This was my question. If nothing is by accident and nothing by chance, as I truly believe, then why had I created this situation? For years I have been teaching that the metaphysical precedes the physical, so what was the metaphysical cause of all this? I would like to say that I became a shining example of deep metaphysical exploration, but the truth is I was so emotionally wrung-out, so drained, that I was lost in despair.

It was at this stage I asked my mentor, the Master Hilarion for insight into what was happening. His reply went something like this: *You have the potential within you to enter the third age, a time of experiencing and sharing with humanity deeper insights into life. This could continue for decades. But—why is there always a but?—you cannot do this the way you are now. This is a potential, not a guarantee. When Michael walked out long ago, and Mixael walked in, you continued with the same body, but you are a different soul. Over the years you have adjusted to this. However, while a few walk-ins are able to make a clean detachment from the person who departed, most are not able to do this. You have adjusted well, and this would have been enough for a normal lifetime, but normal is not your path. Michael was/is a strong, determined character, and inclined toward aggression. Mixael is far more powerful, but is non-aggressive and favours <u>allowing</u> things to happen. Michael would <u>make</u> things happen.*

After owning and living in the body for almost fifty years, there is a very deep cellular imprint of Michael within the body. Even though these cells have died and been replaced many times, the imprint of Michael's consciousness remains. It is within Mixael's power to simply erase this imprint, but it would be a form of violence and he will not do this.

You will be aware that Michael's path was pain and suffering. When change was needed he would create pain and suffering to break him down to the point of no resistance. He did this before his spiritual enlightenment, and this pattern also continued after he had departed the body, when you experienced the shock and grief of losing your first wife. This was so sudden and unexpected that you had no defence. However, it was this that led to your experience of unconditional Love . . . and you finally accepted the reality of Mixael.

This pattern is repeating itself once more, hopefully for the last time. As Mixael, you have chosen to allow the process. This means that you do not fight the pain. It means that you need to focus on the Love and Light of who you are, rather than dialoging with despair and suffering. You need to know that this too, will pass. In many ways, you are fighting the pain and suffering while believing that you are not fighting it. This hinders and prolongs the process. Surrender to it and accept the process, knowing that the final outcome is for your own benefit. Neither should you belittle the process, as it could be fatal. You are experiencing a type of metamorphosis, from Michael to the full expression of Mixael.

Be consciously involved in this process. It is your own evolution.

So it continues. I am learning lesson after lesson on an almost daily basis. I am learning how the mind can play old games while you think you are engaging the new. I am learning that emotions attach even while you are detaching from old emotions. But—and this is a good one!—I am on the road to full recovery. The Mora machine and its therapy is working for me. In some ways the machine is rather like a meeting place between Chinese medicine and homeopathy, although this is just my way of seeing it. The worst is behind me, this I know. I have a fair way to go yet, but I will get there. Mind you, I have no idea what awaits me. As Hilarion said, there is no guarantee. I am learning over and over that this moment is enough.

I cannot help but see that my own personal process which, in all fairness could justifiably be called the Dark Night of the Soul, is the same, or a very similar process that humanity is currently going though. Seldom, maybe never, have so many people lived in such fear and terror, starvation, desperation and homelessness as in these times.

Most countries are experiencing internal strife and even warfare, with violence, rage and anger. Just as with me, the old is being broken down as the Earth energies rise. All humanity is involved in a rare, once in a thousand, maybe ten thousand lifetimes event. On offer is a quantum leap in consciousness. I say on offer, because we can refuse it. We can dig in our heels and attach ourselves even more firmly in the old past, to our useless beliefs, our old grudges and hates.

This is a time when every human is making a choice; the old or the new. It is a choice of either letting go or hanging on. It is a time of either learning to focus on Love and Light, or to cling to the old shadows of despair.

We are being powerfully swept up in times of Change. Love is the new paradigm. The energy of Love that is sweeping over our planet is lifting the frequency of life on Earth. This is a galactic event. We are not alone. The times of corruption and control are finished. The times of self-sovereignty and freedom are being ushered in. This is the long awaited metamorphosis of humanity. We are ready to leave the chrysalis of the old and to fly on the wings of Light into the New. And long have we waited!

I will leave you with a Truth. Whether we accept it or not, believe it or not, live it or not, every human is a magnificent, metaphysical, multidimensional, immortal, eternal Being of Love - the power of creation and Light - the illumination of eternity. Let this be your daily focus. Where you focus your energy flows, and connects, and creates.

Finally, for at least three decades I have been writing and speaking about the power of Love. So I will finish this book in the way I end all of Michael's Musings on social media.

"CONSCIOUSLY . . . choose, live and be, LOVE."

About Michael J. Roads

I am known as a modern mystic. Over many years I have gained a wealth of metaphysical experiences which offer me the most extraordinary insights into life. As a spiritual teacher, I have devised many inner exercises which allow people to experience the interconnectedness of All life, bridging the illusion of separation between our inner and outer worlds. I offer people the ability to maintain a state of inner peace and freedom, regardless of the situations and circumstances of their lives.

Yes . . . this is possible!

All is possible within the power of unconditional Love. I have the consciousness and ability to empower people, thus assisting them in remembering and reconnecting with their own Divine potential.

When certain universal principles of Truth become an aspect of your life, the extraordinary becomes really quite ordinary. Aeons ago, we settled for life in the illusion. I will teach you the way out. I have spent five decades exploring the higher realms of consciousness. It is time for your outdated and outmoded personal world reality to give way to the higher potential of a far Greater Reality.

~ Michael J Roads, Queensland, Australia

For more information please visit Michael's website:
www.michaelroads.com

SixDegreesPublishingGroup.Com

Books that transcend the ordinary.

Milton Keynes UK
Ingram Content Group UK Ltd.
UKHW011911030823
426294UK00002B/135